SQUARE
ONE
BACK TO THE
BASICS

Adam McClendon

Matt Kimbrough

ELECTIO PUBLISHING
first century principles.
a twenty-first century approach.

Square One: Back to the Basics
By Adam McClendon and Matt Kimbrough

Copyright 2018 by Adam McClendon and Matt Kimbrough. All rights reserved.
Cover Design by eLectio Publishing.

ISBN-13: 978-1-63213-478-3

Published by eLectio Publishing, LLC
Little Elm, Texas
http://www.eLectioPublishing.com

Printed in the United States of America

5 4 3 2 1 eLP 22 21 20 19 18

The eLectio Publishing creative team is comprised of: Kaitlyn Campbell, Emily Certain, Lori Draft, Court Dudek, Jim Eccles, Sheldon James, and Christine LePorte.

Publisher's Note

The publisher does not have any control over and does not assume any responsibility for author or third-party websites or their content.

DEDICATION

Along the way, many have contributed to this book by teaching, encouraging, and helping me. My (Matt's) wife, Emily, is a model partner who helps me see with different eyes. Her patience with me and extra care for our young family have added hours to my life, without which my chapters would not exist. My two children, Rylie and Koen, have been the instruments God has used to grow me most significantly over the past four years. My Springhill Baptist Church family is the soil from which this book has grown. Serving the Springhill family is a joy to me because it models what the family of God should be. Finally, I am thankful for the unending patience of our God, who deserves all of the credit for any work of transformation that results from the pages of this book. To God be the glory.

I (Adam) am grateful for so many people. My wife has been an amazing source of encouragement and support throughout our many years of marriage. My children have graciously allowed me to use our lives as an illustration for others to learn. Springhill Baptist Church listened to and lived out these truths in inspirational ways. Dr. Monte Shanks read over my rough drafts and provided significant feedback in the writing of this book. But most of all, like Matt, I'm in awe of God's grace and mercy. May he use this book to help many "grow in the grace and knowledge of our Lord and Savior Jesus Christ" (2 Peter 3:18).

CONTENTS

INTRODUCTION

When I (Matt) got my driver's license, I didn't yet own a cell phone, much less a GPS. So, if I wanted to go somewhere unfamiliar, especially if it was out of state, I would get out a map and come up with a plan. Siri didn't pick my route. I did. And I had to set my course before I ever put the keys in the ignition. One advantage of this archaic system was that I knew my path. I wasn't always waiting for an app to tell me where to turn. There were no surprises.

These days, I travel like everyone else. After I get in the car, I type in the address of my destination and wait for the friendly computerized voice to boss me around. Every once in a while, though, there is a lag. I'll miss an exit because Siri waits until the last second, and I'm in the wrong lane. Even worse, sometimes I lose the signal and find myself stranded alone in unfamiliar terrain. In those moments, I wonder why I didn't just make a plan before I left the house.

The reason we wrote the book you hold in your hands is to provide a roadmap for you. Maybe you're considering becoming a Christian. Maybe you're simply asking questions about Jesus, the church, or the Christian journey. Or, maybe you're a long-time believer who needs a refresher on what it looks like to follow Jesus. No matter where you're starting, we hope to lay out your path before you move any further.

The book is called *Square One* because we want to start with the basics. Switching metaphors, we hope to provide a foundation upon which your church can continue to build. We don't cover every theological question you might have. We don't work through all difficult Bible passages. Instead, this book is designed to be an introduction to Christian faith and practice.

We begin in chapter one with the Gospel story, the starting point of the Christian journey. In chapter two, we discuss the result of the Gospel: a new status before God. The third chapter introduces God's call on our lives to be holy in light of his work in us. Chapter four addresses a major question for any worldview: what is the purpose of life? We argue that each of us exists to glorify God. In the fifth chapter, we look at our new identity as a believer and see how it shapes every part of life. Chapter six demonstrates God's promise to empower his people to obey and honor him. Then, in chapter seven, we ask where the Christian's primary allegiance lies and suggest that Christ should be the center of all. Chapters eight and nine consider the believer's relationship with others. First, chapter eight calls the Christian to a global mission, taking the truth of the Gospel to all people. Then, chapter nine shows the critical importance of the family of God: the church. Finally, chapter ten closes with a look to the future when Christ will return.

If possible, we recommend you read this book in the company of others. Whether you use this book in a classroom, a small group setting, or somewhere else, the insights and guidance of others will prove beneficial. In order to facilitate discussion, we include questions for reflection at the end of each chapter. We also encourage you to dive into the Bible passages we discuss. Don't let this book replace the role of Scripture in your life. If anything, our hope is that each chapter pushes you deeper and deeper into the Bible.

Finally, as you read, know that we are praying for you. We care about the readers of this book. So, we ask God to guide you as you jump into the car and begin this journey with him. We pray that God proves himself to you, transforms you, encourages you, and draws you near. And we pray for God's great blessing on your life as you start with square one.

CHAPTER 1
STORY: REDEEMED BY GOD

God's Story

> *"For God so loved the world that he gave his one and only*
> *Son, that whoever believes in him shall not perish but have*
> *eternal life."*

John 3:16

Everyone loves good stories, and the Bible is full of them. Stories of unbelievable betrayal, gruesome murder, intriguing sensuality, violent rebellion, fierce battles, tremendous faith, supernatural beings, and supernatural healings are all found in the Bible, but these stories are really subcomponents of the ultimate storyline of the Bible.[1] The Bible is a collection of books and letters telling the story of God rescuing people from sin. God's means of rescuing people from sin and restoring them to a right relationship with himself is called the "Good News" or the "Gospel." That's what this chapter is about. It's about understanding God's redemptive story and where we fit into it.

"How does someone get to heaven?" What answer do you think most other people would give? Madelyn, my (Adam's) oldest daughter, was five-years-old when we were sitting outside a store

Non-believers, believers, or both

---

[1]Using the word "stories" is not intended to imply that these events are not real. "Stories" simply picks up on the fact that the various authors of the various books of the Bible often use historical narratives to communicate to the audience.

waiting for Mommy to run in and get a loaf of bread.[2] Since we were active in our church, had family devotions regularly, and talked about God with other people in front of our children, I wanted to see her level of understanding. So I asked her, "Madelyn, how is someone saved?" She looked at me, almost confused, and calmly said, "They fight back."[3] Smiling, I responded, "Well, sure, if someone is in trouble that person would need to fight back, but I'm asking, 'How does someone go to heaven?'" "They die," she stated emphatically with a look on her face that clearly communicated that as an adult I should already know these things. I started laughing, and then we began to have a great conversation about the nature of God and his plan for getting us to heaven.

Over the years, I've had the opportunity to have a lot of spiritual conversations with people. Many of the people I talk to about spiritual truths believe they will get to heaven by being "good", or at least "good enough." When I ask those people why they think their morality can save them, they often tell me they have just always been taught that way or that it just seems to make sense to them. Many of these same individuals believe the question of how to get to heaven is important and believe the Bible is true, but they have never looked in the Bible personally to see how God answers the question. Why not? If the Bible is true, then what it says about how to have a relationship with God and go to heaven is pretty significant and worth investigating. I mean, think about it. Many, if not most, of these same people would not even buy a computer without doing a little research by referencing consumer reports or looking up customer satisfaction ratings, yet they are banking the eternal destiny of their souls on some general assumptions and various inconclusive conversations.

[2] The names of people used in this book for illustrative purposes have been changed with the exception of family members.

[3] This conversation illustrates how we tend to use "churchy" language without taking into consideration what other people hear. My five-year-old naturally understood that for someone to be save (i.e. rescued) that person would need to fight back.

4

What about you? Where are you in your understanding of God's story? Whether you know the gospel well or not, the gospel is always relevant and should encourage us. So, let's take some time together and walk through the story of God's plan in the Bible. We'll see that he is a holy and just God who has provided a way for us to have a relationship with him and experience eternal life.

God's Perfection

What is the characteristic of God most people would mention if they were asked to describe Him? From my experience, the love of God is nearly always and almost exclusively mentioned. God is love, and he extends his love to us. He is infinitely more loving than we are, and numerous verses support this truth. Psalm 63:3 says, "Because your love is better than life, my lips will glorify you." However, he is also a loving God who is perfect in his justice and holiness. Focusing on God's love without rightly considering God's justice and holiness devalues the story. We must remember the mantra that the creatures of heaven declare over the throne of God is not "love, love, love" but "holy, holy, holy, is the Lord God Almighty, who was, and is, and is to come" (Rev. 4:8b).

Look at what the last part of Leviticus 19:2 commands: "Be holy because I, the LORD your God, am holy." Because God is holy and perfect, he cannot and will not tolerate or be at peace with sin. In other words, God treats sin as an enemy of his perfect holiness, and since he is holy, he commands anyone who desires to have a relationship with him to be holy.

This point is proven time and time again in the Bible.

> "'Do not come any closer,' God said. 'Take off your sandals, for the place where you are standing is holy ground'"
>
> Exodus 3:5

> "I am the LORD your God; consecrate yourselves and be holy, because I am holy…I am the LORD who brought you up out of Egypt to be your God; therefore be holy, because I am holy.
>
> Leviticus 11:44a, 45

[Handwritten margin note, top right: "Not very good, probably about a 3 out of 10. Sadly"]

[Handwritten margin note, right: "God is not just Love but Holy and Just"]

"But the LORD Almighty will be exalted by his justice, and the holy God will be proved holy by his righteous acts"

Isaiah 5:16

"For I am the LORD your God, the Holy One of Israel, your Savior..."

?

Isaiah 43:3

"For your Maker is your husband—the LORD Almighty is his name—the Holy One of Israel is your Redeemer; he is called the God of all the earth"

(Isaiah 54:5).

"Therefore, since we have these promises, dear friends, let us purify ourselves from everything that contaminates body and spirit, perfecting holiness out of reverence for God"

2 Corinthians 7:1

"For God did not call us to be impure, but to live a holy life"

1 Thessalonians 4:7

"Make every effort to live in peace with everyone and to be holy; without holiness no one will see the Lord"

Hebrews 12:14

"But just as he who called you is holy, so be holy in all you do; for it is written: 'Be holy, because I am holy'"

1 Peter 1:15–16

"All who has this hope in him purify themselves, just as he is pure"

1 John 3:3

If we want a relationship with God Almighty, then we must acknowledge him as he has revealed himself to us. He is holy. He is perfect.

God's Problem

"Houston, we have a problem." If God is holy and perfect, and if God commands anyone who desires to have a relationship with him to be holy and perfect, then who can have a relationship with God? After all, we are sinful, right? Romans 3:23 declares "all have sinned and fall short of the glory of God." But let's say you are better than the average person. After all, you're not that bad. You haven't drowned kittens in a pool, murdered anyone, or desecrated a cemetery. Isn't this how we tend to think? But such thinking is what gets us into trouble. We tend to compare ourselves to those around us versus looking at God's own word and evaluating ourselves based on his standard: his own perfection. It's as if we think that God grades on a bell curve, and as long as we are ahead of the curve, we'll be okay. So, our standard for acceptance becomes those around us rather than God's perfection. Because God is holy, he cannot stand in a right relationship with anyone who is not holy. God's very nature demands that we be holy to have a relationship with him. So, even the smallest of sins we commit contaminates this relationship. Sin brings us under condemnation before God.

Take the Ten Commandments as God's most basic standard. Have you ever lied? Lusted? Coveted? Dishonored a parent? You may seek to justify your behavior by other standards, but by God's standards, you have sinned. Just one sin blemishes the record so you cannot be considered holy. You deserve judgment.

Wait! Hold the press! That's the part that loses a lot of people. "Are you saying that one little sin deserves eternal estrangement and punishment? But I'm *not* as bad as so many others. What kind of God would condemn me based on such insignificant sin?" A holy God. Our sin only seems insignificant to us when compared to our own cultural values and to those around us, but when we examine sin against the backdrop of a perfectly holy God, it is altogether different. The idea that one sin causes imperfection and keeps us from God is hard for many of us to believe. We don't seem to have a hard time believing that we are sinful; rather, we seem to have a hard time believing our sin is really that big of a deal. Culture has

7

done a masterful job of minimizing certain sins, particularly those more culturally acceptable. Our culture tells us to use others as our comparative standard, rather than God and his holiness. Arguing that a little sin isn't that bad is like arguing a little Ebola doesn't hurt. We need to understand that any degree of sin contaminates the entirety of the person.

Reread what happened to Adam and Eve in the Garden of Eden lest there be any misunderstanding of the truth that the smallest sin creates a death sentence in our relationship with God and brings us into judgment (Gen. 2–3). Adam is created in Genesis and placed in the garden. The LORD gives unbelievable freedom to Adam with only one prohibition: "You are free to eat from any tree in the garden; but you must not eat from the tree of the knowledge of good and evil, for when you eat of it you will surely die" (Gen. 2:16–17). Later, when Adam and Eve sin by eating the fruit, they are judged, thrown out of Eden, and the entire world is cursed—plagued by evil, disorder, and chaos. All of this destruction over eating a piece of forbidden fruit! Wow! When we read that, it honestly feels incredibly harsh to us, maybe even too harsh, so we have a tendency to gloss over the real implication, which is that God cannot stand in a right relationship with sin. Ignoring sin a violation of God's very character and nature. Sin brings condemnation and death, and just in case we miss it in Genesis, God reaffirms this principle later, telling us in Ezekiel, "The soul who sins is the one who will die" (18:4b).

Sin separates people from God. So, to find salvation and be reconciled to God, we have to acknowledge that we cannot do it on our own. After all, good works do not undo bad works. This thought is another one with which we often struggle. We have a tendency to believe that if we are good enough, it might make up for the bad things we have done, even though this idea doesn't match our reality of justice or the biblical teachings of salvation. The fact is that, once we have sinned, the damage has been done damage we cannot reverse on our own. Here is an example to illustrate the point that sin creates a permanent stain. Imagine that you are taking a

1000-question test. Let's say you miss only one question. Did you make a perfect score? Is your test perfect? No. Now, let's imagine that 1000 more questions are added to the test, and you get every one of those correct. Is your score perfect now? No. Regardless of how many more questions are answered correctly, if one answer is wrong, the score is no longer perfect. Getting right answers does not undo the answers we miss. The same is true for our lives. Good works do not make up for sinful actions. Here's another example. Let's say you have a brand new white bed sheet. It's pristine. As you lay it out over your bed, you get a call and leave the room. When you return, your first grader is sitting in the middle of the sheet laying out her school supplies, including her permanent marker. The lid is off, and you see a huge, unbleachable stain where the marker has bled onto the sheet. Now, you can sew as much new white fabric to the edges as you wish, but it will not undo the fact that there is a huge stain in the middle of the sheet. Adding material around the stain doesn't remove the stain. The stain has to be covered or cut out. In the same way, adding good works does not pay for our bad works.

Let's think of it from a legal perspective to see how we recognize this truth naturally. Could you imagine someone standing before a judge for murder and saying, "Yes, I did it, Judge, but I've also done a lot of good things in my life. I've obeyed the speed limit. I've paid my taxes. I've never robbed a liquor store." What will that judge say? "Oh, well, in that case, you're free to go." No, or else that judge would be an unjust judge. Instead, a just judge will say, "That doesn't matter. The court expects you to obey the law. Your obedience doesn't undo your disobedience. You are guilty!" The same applies to God, who is the perfect standard and creator of righteousness, holiness, and justice. If God overlooked evil because of some good we did, he would not be just. The reality is that our works are insufficient to pay for our sin. We are sinful and deserving of judgment. So, what's the solution?

Ask for forgiveness

9

God's Provision

The whole idea of a salvation implies being saved from something bad. That's why the Bible refers to the message of salvation as good news (the gospel). God has bridged the chasm that separates us from him. He has solved our unsolvable problem. He accomplished for us what we could not accomplish for ourselves. Considering this point, several questions should be addressed.

First, what has God provided salvation from? He provides salvation from the bondage and penalty sin brought.[4]

> *"For the wages of sin is death, but the gift of God is eternal life in Christ Jesus our Lord."*
>
> Romans 6:23

> *"What a wretched man I am! Who will rescue me from this body that is subject to death? Thanks be to God, who delivers me through Jesus Christ our Lord! So then, I myself in my mind am a slave to God's law, but in my sinful nature a slave to the law of sin."*
>
> Romans 7:24–25

Sin brings with it death and bondage. Both spiritual death and physical death are ultimate consequences of our sin. In contrast, the life that Jesus brings is spiritual and physical. Our lives are spiritually transformed here and physically transformed in the kingdom of heaven when we pass from this sinful world into his presence. In the kingdom of heaven, our bodies will be made perfect, and the impact of sin's curse will be destroyed.

Second, how did God provide salvation from the death and bondage of sin? Time and time again in the Old Testament, sacrifices are described and required. Why? One reason is these sacrifices revealed that sins can only be paid for by the shedding of perfect, innocent blood.

---

[4]For another example of being in bondage to sin, see Peter's remarks to Simon in Acts 8:21–23.

"In fact, the law requires that nearly everything be cleansed with blood, and without the shedding of blood there is no forgiveness"

(handwritten: Jesus dying for our sins)

Hebrews 9:22

Another reason is that these Old Testament sacrifices point to Jesus as the ultimate perfect Lamb of God who takes away the sins of those who trust in him.

"'Look, the Lamb of God, who takes away the sin of the world!'"

John 1:29b

Throughout the Bible, God demonstrates that he is both loving and holy. In his holiness, however, he cannot tolerate sin and must judge it, but, because of his love, he provides a way for us to receive forgiveness and cleansing from it in order to be restored to a right relationship with him. God provided the path for restoration by sending Jesus Christ, the Lamb of God, to die on a cross and be raised from the grave as our sacrifice for sin. That's why the Apostle Paul writes to the church at Corinth, "By this gospel you are saved…For what I received I passed on to you as of first importance: that Christ died for our sins according to the Scriptures, that he was buried, that he was raised on the third day according to the Scriptures" (1 Cor. 15:2–4). Elsewhere, Jesus himself proclaims, "I am the way and the truth and the life. No one comes to the Father except through me" (John 14:6b). Jesus is the perfect and final sacrifice for sin. Because of God's holiness, he judges sin, and because of his love and grace, he provides Jesus, who takes our judgment upon himself so that you and I can be restored to a right relationship with God the Father. We can be forgiven through Jesus. Here are a few more verses revealing God's provision through Jesus as the only path to salvation from sin's curse.

(handwritten margin: Jesus died so that we live. He was true sacrifice.)

"But God demonstrates his own love for us in this: While we were still sinners, Christ died for us."

Romans 5:8

11

> *"'Salvation is found in no one else [but Jesus], for there is no other name under heaven given to mankind by which we must be saved.'"*

> Acts 4:12

That's one reason why the Bible calls salvation a "new birth" (John 3:3, 5, 7). It is a removal of sin and the beginning of a new relationship, a new life, with God. Thus, the perfect provision from God for providing deliverance from sin and restoring our relationship with God is the death and resurrection of Jesus the Messiah.

Third, what must I do to receive this provision for my sin? Initially, it may be helpful to talk about *how we do not receive this provision*. Salvation is

- ❖ Not praying a prayer.
- ❖ Not walking an aisle at church.
- ❖ Not going to church.
- ❖ Not being baptized. *Have not been baptized yet.*
- ❖ Not having Christian parents. *? What if you don't?*
- ❖ Not a simple acknowledgment of Christ's deity, sacrificial death, and resurrection.

This last point may be the hardest for many "church" people. Notice what God's Word in James reveals. "You believe that there is one God. Good! Even the demons believe that—and shudder" (James 2:19). It is not enough to simply acknowledge the truth. You must accept God's free gift of salvation and give your life to Jesus. That is why the Bible mentions faith and repentance together as the requirement to experience this new life (Acts 20:21). The new life is available but can only be received by a repentant heart of faith.

Let's try and explain biblical faith this way. Suppose you see a parachute. You can believe the object is a parachute (recognition). You can even believe that the parachute works (acknowledgment). However, that is entirely different than putting on the parachute, going up 15,000 feet, and jumping out of a plane with the parachute as the only means of salvation (trust). In other words, trusting solely in Jesus. That's biblical faith! To receive salvation takes an exercise of repentant faith in which you trust solely in Jesus' work on the cross to save you from sin. Repentant faith is recognizing that you are a guilty sinner with no hope, rejecting sin, and placing your trust entirely in Jesus' work on your behalf. Faith is the means of receiving God's gracious gift of salvation. Salvation comes from believing on the Lord Jesus Christ as your sole means of deliverance from the condemnation and bondage of sin.

> *"He then brought them out and asked, 'Sirs, what must I do to be saved?' They replied, 'Believe in the Lord Jesus, and you will be saved—you and your household.'"*

Acts 16:30–31

It is repentant faith that changes one's life. It is faith that bends one's knee in allegiance to King Jesus (Phil. 2:9–11). It is believing that he provides salvation and surrendering one's will to his. In other words, true biblical faith is a deep-seated belief that *results* in a changed life.

All of this brings up a final question. Where do good works fit in? Works are a part of salvation. Good works should be a necessary byproduct of a grateful heart, which has experienced salvation. Thus, if you truly receive this gracious provision God has made for your sin in Christ, then you will seek to live for him, not to receive the gift but because it has already been given. You will strive to live for him out of a deep appreciation for what he has done for you (Rom 6:11–14; Eph 2:10). Doesn't this idea make sense? Imagine being in a horrible accident on the interstate. As the metal collapses around you, you are pinned in the car. Suddenly, you smell the toxic concoction of burning fuel, rubber, and plastic. "Oh no! The car is on fire." Only seconds before the flames will engulf you and extinguish your life, someone dives into the car, frees your pinned legs, and carries you to safety. How hard would it be for you to honor them? How hard would it be for you to fulfill a request they might have?

[handwritten: And Jesus saved ours so he is our Hero ↓]

Not hard at all. Why? Because that person is your hero and saved your life. When we understand the extent of the rescue, compliance with requests is not arduous *[handwritten: Hard]* but easy. And, his commands should not feel burdensome to us; rather, they should be understood as guidelines by which we as the people of God can experience joyful, abundant, Spirit-filled, blessed living (1 John 5:2–5). Considering these things, let's look at the promise that exists for all who trust in God's provision for sin.

God's Promise

[handwritten: Gods consideration for your eternity]

God promises to reconcile to himself all who trust in Jesus and give them eternal life. God's provision for sin through Jesus is not automatically applied, but it is freely offered. Don't let this point go unnoticed. God's promise of salvation is conditioned upon reception. Romans 10:9–10 reiterates the idea that the provision of God must be received. The text reads, "That if you declare with your mouth, 'Jesus is Lord,' and believe in your heart that God raised him from the dead, you will be saved. For it is with your heart that you believe and are justified, and it is with your mouth that you profess your faith and are saved." Did you catch that second word, "if"? That's an important "if." Only those who receive God's provision for sin experience a restored relationship with God and are saved from sin's condemnation and penalty (Rom. 6:23; 8:1).

[handwritten margin: My answer to Page 3]

God issues a promise for those who trust in his provision for sin. The promise is for anyone of any race, gender, social class, background, sexual orientation, or behavior who acknowledges the holiness of God, the egregiousness of sin, and trusts in the sole-sufficient provision of Jesus' death and resurrection to atone for sin. Anyone who does this in repentant faith will be restored to a right relationship with God, adopted as a spiritual son or daughter, and given an eternal heavenly home to abide with him forever. So, let's talk more about this beautiful promise together and look at how it is repeated from different perspectives over and over again in the Bible.

[handwritten margin: Anyone!]

God promises to free us from the condemnation and bondage of sin.

> "'Come now, let us settle the matter,' says the LORD. 'Though your sins are like scarlet, they shall be as white as snow; though they are red as crimson, they shall be like wool.'"

> Isaiah 1:18

> "We all, like sheep, have gone astray, each of us has turned to our own way; and the LORD has laid on him the iniquity of us all."

> Isaiah 53:6

> "'All the prophets testify about him [Jesus] that everyone who believes in him receives forgiveness of sins through his name.'"

> Acts 10:43

> "God made him [Jesus] who had no sin to be sin for us, so that in him we might become the righteousness of God."

> 2 Corinthians 5:21

> "He himself [Jesus] bore our sins in his body on the cross, so that we might die to sins and live for righteousness; by his wounds you have been healed."

> 1 Peter 2:24

Sin's guilt and stain are removed through Jesus' sacrifice, making those who trust in him clean before God the Father.

God promises to be our heavenly Father and adopt us as one of his children for eternity. Moreover, with our adoption by God, we receive special rights, privileges, and an inheritance that belong to the children of our heavenly Father.

> "Yet to all who received him [Jesus], to those who believed in his name, he gave the right to become children of God."

> John 1:12

15

"For those who are led by the Spirit of God are the children of God. The Spirit you received does not make you slaves, so that you live in fear again; rather, the Spirit you received brought about your adoption to sonship. And by him we cry, 'Abba, Father.' The Spirit himself testifies with our spirit that we are God's children. Now if we are children, then we are heirs—heirs of God and co-heirs with Christ, if indeed we share in his sufferings in order that we may also share in his glory."

Romans 8:14–17

"Now that this faith has come, we are no longer under a guardian. So in <u>Christ Jesus you are all children of God through faith.</u>"

Galatians 3:25–26

God promises to secure us in his love for an everlasting abundant life with him in heaven.

"'I [Jesus] have come that they may have life, and have it to the full...I give them eternal life, and they shall never perish; no one will snatch them out of my hand.'"

John 10:10b, 28

"Who shall separate us from the love of Christ? Shall trouble or hardship or persecution or famine or nakedness or danger or sword?...No, in all these things we are more than conquerors through him who loved us. For I am convinced that neither death nor life, neither angels nor demons, neither the present nor the future, nor any powers, neither height nor depth, nor anything else in all creation, will be able to separate us from the love of God that is in Christ Jesus our Lord."

Romans 8:35, 37–39

"And the God of all grace, who called you to his eternal glory in Christ, after you have suffered a little while, will himself restore you and make you strong, firm and steadfast."

1 Peter 5:10

"I write these things to you who believe in the name of the Son of God so that you may know that you have eternal life."

1 John 5:13

An Invitation

Have you had your relationship with the eternal God of the universe restored? Are you his child, and is he your God? Have you trusted in the sacrifice of Jesus as payment and cleansing for your sins? Do you have peace regarding the afterlife? Or do you still feel the enslavement, shame, and turmoil of sin?

Maybe you prayed a prayer when you were a child, but it was uninformed and not accompanied by repentant faith. Maybe you walked an aisle at a church but never really trusted in Jesus and repented of your sins. Maybe you were born into a Christian family but never personally made Jesus your Savior and Lord. Maybe you have not heard this message before or have heard but refused to believe. Yet something is different this time. Perhaps for the first time, you see the truth of God's provision and his promise of eternal life, and you want to be saved.

Trust in his provision today. That's it. Exercise repentant faith. Repent acknowledging that you have sinned against a holy God and stand condemned. Believe Jesus died and rose again as payment for your own sins, and trust him as your Savior and Lord. But understand that you are trusting exclusively in Jesus as the sole means of forgiveness for your sins.

For those have trusted in Jesus as the provision to be restored to God and have claimed the promises of this incredible invitation, are

17

you encouraged? Do you see the continued relevance of the gospel in your life? Does God's amazing love and grace motivate you to live more faithfully for him, not in order to earn salvation, but out of thanksgiving for your salvation? When you fall into sin, does it cripple your life or serve as a humble reminder as to why you still need the good news of Jesus' provision? As believers in Jesus the Christ, we should always remember the amazing grace of God extended to us. We must fight not to become so familiar with this incredible story that it fails to move our souls, stir our emotions, and make us thankful. We must be careful not to somehow fall into the trap of believing that we are good on our own. We must remember that any righteousness now found in our lives, any victory over sin and evil, is a testament to the redeeming work of God in transforming our hearts and minds by the power of his Holy Spirit.

Finally, we must, as Christians, remember that there is a world lost in sin and looking for hope. We must realize that we are on a rescue mission for God. The world in which we live needs to know grace, and we are the means that God has chosen for taking this undeserved message to it (Rom. 10:14–15). Whether you have just trusted in Jesus as your Savior or have been a believer for decades, when was the last time you shared this story of God's redemptive work with someone? Maybe you want to but just aren't sure how. May I suggest trying a little experiment? Would you try two things?

First, I'm asking you to pray. Pray a very simple prayer: "God, would you open an opportunity for me to share your story with someone? When this opportunity comes, help me to recognize it and then have the courage to share your story with them graciously."

Secondly, here is a technique I've found helpful in opening opportunities. It involves asking only two questions. In the course of a conversation when it seems appropriate, say, "You know, I've been reading the Bible, thinking about some things it reveals, and wanted to ask your opinion." Then ask a version of these two questions. "Do you believe that there is a heaven?" After they answer, follow up with "How do you think someone gets there?" Listen carefully, and engage with them in casual conversation. If this

18

story of God's saving grace is an important part of your life, it doesn't have to be awkward or forced. It should be a casual conversation. If the door closes and the person isn't interested, that's okay, but more often than not, if approached graciously, casually, and conversationally, you'll find that people are more open than you often give them credit.

Questions for reflection: Anwsered in my notebook

1 How familiar are you with the story of God presented in this chapter? What parts have you heard before? What was new?

Not very familiar, I've heard what I would call the basics. A lot was new to be honest.

2 Is there a Bible passage used in the chapter that stood out to you? What was it, and why did it make such an impact? *Page 6 saying your maker is your husband. It stood out because it just comes to show how he is everything*

3 What is the holiness of God? How does it affect the way we relate to God? *?*

4 How does this chapter define belief and repentant faith? What is the difference between them?

5 After reading the chapter, how would you define the Gospel? How would you summarize "the story" for someone else?

6 What is the right response to the Gospel for an unbeliever? In what ways does the Gospel story continue to impact people who are saved?

7 Who are three people you know that need to hear the Gospel story this week?

CHAPTER 2
STATUS: RECONCILED TO GOD

Digging Deeper

But now apart from the law the righteousness of God has been made known, to which the Law and the Prophets testify. This righteousness is given through faith in Jesus Christ to all who believe. There is no difference between Jew and Gentile, for all have sinned and fall short of the glory of God, and all are justified freely by his grace through the redemption that came by Christ Jesus. God presented Christ as a sacrifice of atonement, through the shedding of his blood—to be received by faith. He did this to demonstrate his righteousness, because in his forbearance he had left the sins committed beforehand unpunished—he did it to demonstrate his righteousness at the present time, so as to be just and the one who justifies those who have faith in Jesus.

Romans 3:21–26

We discussed this story God has given us called "the gospel" in the last chapter.

In short, the gospel (or good news) is that Jesus lived a perfect life, died on a cross, and rose again for my sin so that if I believe in him, I will have eternal life. The Apostle Paul summarizes the gospel this way: "For what I received I passed on to you as of first importance: that Christ died for our sins according to the Scriptures, that he was buried, that he was raised on the third day according to the Scriptures" (1 Cor. 15:3–4). The Apostle John, in what may be the most famous verse in the Bible, declares, "For God so loved the world that he gave his one and only Son, that whoever believes in him shall not perish but have eternal life" (John 3:16). This is our story.

This chapter shifts the focus a little to discuss our status, particularly, what it means to be justified. But why? Why go any further than the basics of the gospel? After all, isn't the gospel the most important thing? Shouldn't we just talk about the good news? Why explain more? Why not move on to the important stuff like the book of Revelation? Why use big words like "justification"?

These words, such as justification, refer to great promises and important concepts with respect to living for God. They are not just fancy words. Their meanings matter, and it is important that we understand them. A few years ago, I (Adam) was teaching a Bible study through the book of Philippians. During the study of Philippians 3:12, in a conversation about justification and sanctification, a man spoke up and asked, "Why do we have to be so complicated? It's all just about Jesus. Why do we have to learn about these big words?" "Well," I responded, "we need to remember that God put these big words in the Bible. Since he put them there, we need to learn what they mean so that we can understand what he wants to tell us and how he wants us to live."

The Bible is all about Jesus. That truth should encourage Christ followers to press even deeper into the entire council of God's word and not stop with the simplest understanding possible (Heb. 5:12-14). Because the Bible is all about Jesus, believers are to be driven by the story of the cross to the rest of Scripture. The Bible stirs the child of God to adore Jesus. The Bible explains what it means to live with and for Jesus. The Bible shows how Jesus transforms the life of believers and how Jesus' second coming provides hope and motivation for the Christian life. All these flow from the reality of Jesus' life and work. God encourages us through his word to grow and share his truth in its entirety with the world. That's one reason Jesus challenges all his followers to "go and make disciples of all nations, baptizing them in the name of the Father and of the Son and

Go further & never stop!

of the Holy Spirit, and teaching them to obey everything I have commanded you" (Matt. 28:19-20a). We must not ignore the truth that part of going and winning a lost world to Jesus is also maturing them in Jesus by "teaching them to obey" *all that he has commanded.*

Inexcusable Behavior

To "justify" something means to prove it is right. We are masters at striving to justify our actions, aren't we? Personally, I struggle a lot with sin. I do. I've struggled most recently with anger, worry, anxiety, and fear. These sins reveal themselves in various facets of my life, especially at home. I find myself getting upset and short with the kids, snapping at my wife over little things, and repeatedly harping with little to no grace. Despite lines being crossed, I find myself justifying my behavior. After all, we are in the middle of moving, we are in the midst of changing jobs, and we are busy without a moment to ourselves running from sporting event to sporting event for the children. Plus, I'm doing a lot better than "Bob" over there. It's really no big deal. I mean, these sins aren't really that bad. Who's really getting hurt? And in the wake of all of this self-justification is my family bearing the private brunt of my sin.

A few years ago, my family and I were getting into our minivan. For the ten-thousandth time, our kids were arguing about who was going to sit where. My youngest, Cameron, was standing while arguing with his sisters. I'm trying to back out of the driveway and am completely fed up with all the shenanigans. In frustration, I hit the brakes, which made him sit down, and yelled at the kids. Immediately, I was filled with shame and regret. I knew my attitude and behavior was wrong. At that point, I felt like a complete failure as a Christian parent. I was horribly frustrated and began to back quickly out of the driveway when bam! In all of the confusion, I forgot that my mother-n-law's car was in the driveway. Did I mention it was her *new* car? Did I mention that it was the first car she had ever bought new? I couldn't believe it. In my heart, I was screaming, "If they would have just sat down," but the reality was that I chose to lose my temper, act sinfully, and rush.

[handwritten note:] We all chose things in moments of rage or desperation but what we do after is key and also helps.

[handwritten marginal note:] were all human no matter who we are

The Message in Church 10-6-19 Do we actually owe up to what we've done or do we blame others?

Do you ever seek to justify your attitude or actions? Pause for a minute, and think about how we talk:

You made me so mad.

That ticked me off.

The kids are driving me crazy.

Essentially, we are saying that our bad behavior, our bad emotions, or our bad thoughts are really the inevitable, unavoidable, consequence of someone or something else. We think, "I'm not to blame. It's not my fault. My behavior is justified because my circumstances are worthy of such erratic, idiotic, uncontrolled, emotion-driven behavior."

We also justify other sins such as:

...having a bad attitude and sense of entitlement at home. "I've worked hard all day."

...embezzling at work. "I deserve those reams of paper because they underpay me."

....an affair or unbiblical divorce. "My spouse isn't attentive enough" or "Well, we've just grown apart."

...playing solitaire on the company's dime. "I'm just taking a break."

...neglecting time with God. "I'm swamped."

...ignoring what God has said. "I just don't understand it all."

We are masters at trying to justify our sinful tendencies. While we may fool others and even ourselves at times, we can't fool God! Yet, in God's grace and mercy, he has made a way to justify our sins, not by dismissing them but by paying for them. So, let us walk through Romans 3:21-26 to see God's plan for justifying our sin.

Equal Footing

The Apostle Paul builds an argument throughout the first three chapters of the book of Romans by showing the universal sinfulness of humankind and how everyone is condemned under the law.

Everyone knows they are sinful since their conscience informs them they have sinned. At this point in his writing, he transitioned to speak of the solution for this condemnation. He writes, "But now apart from the law the righteousness of God has been made known, to which the Law and the Prophets testify. This righteousness is given through faith in Jesus Christ to all who believe" (Rom. 3:21-22a).

Part of Paul's point is that the Law and the Prophets, the Old Testament, exist to point us to Jesus Christ. While Jesus is not explicitly revealed by name until the New Testament, the Old Testament consistently alludes to him. These elements of the Old Testament "point to a work of God yet future that would provide humans a way of atonement."[5] These Old Testament passages may not explain the full manifestation of who Jesus is, but they provide a shadow, an imprint, a witness of him. God's righteousness in dealing with sin was foretold in the Old Testament but revealed on the cross.

This righteousness can be experienced, and we too can be declared righteous (justified) through faith in Jesus. It is important to notice two things here: specificity and individual responsibility. First, Jesus is specifically mentioned as the only one through whom we can be made righteous before God. Jesus declared elsewhere what Paul is emphasizing here. As Jesus said, "I am the way and the truth and the life. No one comes to the Father except through me" (John 14:6), so Paul in Romans affirmed that it is only through placing one's faith in the specific person of Jesus Christ that one can be made right before God. A few years ago, a member of the church I pastored was having heart problems and had to go to the emergency room. I received a call, kissed my wife, and headed out. I pulled the hospital up on my maps app since I was new to the area. I drove for about twenty minutes and then "arrived" at my destination. One problem, it was the wrong place. It was a surgical center, not the hospital. I scrambled, found the correct address, and

---

[5]Robert H. Mounce, *Romans*, vol. 27, NAC (Nashville: B&H, 1995), 114.

finally made it; however, to get to the hospital, I ultimately had to get on the "right" road. Any road would not work. I need to be on National Avenue. The same is true spiritually with becoming reconciled to God. All roads do not lead to the same place. God has revealed that to have a relationship with him, to be made right with him, you eventually have to go through Jesus. Abstract belief alone is not sufficient. Effective faith has to trust in the right object: Jesus.

Second, each of us is uniquely responsible for placing our faith in Jesus Christ as the Savior who alone can redeem us from sin and make us right before God the Father. This personal and specific faith is something each one must express to be declared righteous by God. Salvation is only experienced by "those who believe" in the Lord Jesus.

"There is no difference between Jew and Gentile" (Rom. 3:22b). This introductory statement of non-distinction is essential. Don't miss it. Remember, Jews and Gentiles alike are reading this letter, and one group, the Jews, think they are made right with God by being born into covenant with him as a Jew. Paul's statement served as an indictment against those who thought that their ethnicity was superior to others before God. We are not exempt from this presumptuous mistake. Some people may think that God favors them, they are spiritually superior, or they are right before God because—

"I speak in tongues."

"I'm a church member."

"I'm part of those who have been confirmed and baptized in the church."

"I take communion."

"My parents are Christians."

"I belong to a Sunday School class."

"I'm in a youth group."

"I tithe." = Money

"I'm always concerned for the poor and help the helpless."

"I always denounce injustice."

"I'm wealthy and blessed."

"I'm Caucasian, African-American, Hispanic, Jewish, etc."

Not only did Paul's declaration of non-distinction serve as an indictment against those misguided by their dependence on their heritage, like the Jews, but it also conversely served as a great encouragement to the non-Jews, the Gentiles, who were reading Paul's letter. Paul's statement was encouraging in part because it revealed not only that all are equally guilty before God because of their sin but also that God had made a provision for all through faith in Jesus. So, while all are equally condemned, all are equally savable through the saving work of Jesus Christ through his death and resurrection on behalf of sinners. Jesus paid the penalty for the sins of all who believe and trust in him as the substitute for their sin. *Sacrifice*

This truth applies to us even today, regardless of how close or far away from God we might think we are. God made a way for you through Jesus Christ! Maybe you are an active druggie, pedophile, murderer, porn addict, homosexual, embezzler, adulterer, blasphemer, liar, glutton, gossip, etc. *Greedy eater* Your "gross" sins are no more condemning than stealing cookies out of your mom's cookie jar, because God's grace is just as sufficient for all of your sins, whether they are great or small. Paul reiterates this beautiful truth in 1 Corinthians 6:9-11:

Someone who mocks/ derides a religion or claims to be God.

> Or do you not know that wrongdoers will not inherit the kingdom of God? Do not be deceived: Neither the sexually immoral nor idolaters nor adulterers nor men who have sex with men nor thieves nor the greedy nor drunkards nor slanderers nor swindlers will inherit the kingdom of God. And that is what some of you were. But you were washed, you were sanctified, you were justified in the name of the Lord Jesus Christ and by the Spirit of our God.

Washed away but the blood of Jesus.

Regardless of your heritage or how dark, dirty, and desperate your past was, Jesus Christ is the redeemer who can make you right with God and cleanse all sin. When Jesus comes into your life and he cleanses you from sin, God declares you eternally justified in his eyes. He declares you are his child. God cleanses you from all sin—sin from your past as well as those you have yet to commit. He does not leave you in your sin. He changes your status, and as a result, you can now live rightly for him. But I'm getting a little too far ahead at this point since that topic will be discussed in the next chapter. For now, let's see how Paul continued to explain the way one can be justified before God.

Paid in Full

Paul continues his thought by building on his statement of non-distinction to explain his point further: "[F]or all have sinned and fall short of the glory of God, and all are justified freely by his grace through the redemption that came by Christ Jesus" (Rom. 3:23-24). Everyone is guilty and worthy of condemnation before God, regardless of each person's perceived merits. We are only justified through a free gift of grace.

At this point, we need to pause and provide greater clarity concerning the question "What exactly is justification?"

> *Justification is the decisive declaration of God whereby Christ's righteousness is imputed to a sinner as a gracious gift by means of faith, and the sinner's status is declared to be righteous.*

Defined

Let me illustrate it this way. Imagine being in a courtroom and standing before a judge on trial for a crime, a crime that you and the judge know you committed. The judge pronounces the verdict: "Guilty!" Then, at that moment, Jesus comes forward and volunteers to bear the penalty for your crime as your substitute. The court concedes and allows Jesus to bear your punishment. The judge then declares, "Judgment rendered, and judgment has been paid. The plaintiff is now justified before this court, and the requirements of the law fulfilled." This declaration means that you have been made right with the court. Your crime was not absolved but paid for. As a result, your crimes can no longer be held against you. No double jeopardy exists. You are free before the judge. That is what Jesus did

Example of what Jesus did for our sins

for us. He fulfilled the requirements of the law and bore the penalty of the law on behalf of all who would believe and trust in him. Everyone who accepts Jesus as his or her substitute sin-penalty-bearer is declared righteous (justified) before the court of God.

We are made right with God through this declaration, and we are now "justified" (righteous) in God's eyes through Jesus Christ; however, as a result of this new life in Christ, we should become more holy and righteous in character and action. That is the process of progressive sanctification, about which we will discuss more in the next chapter.[6] For this chapter, the point is that Jesus fulfilled the penalty required by our sin, so that if we trust in him as our substitute, we will be justified in God's sight. Everyone who trusts in Jesus as their Savior has his or her status changed from condemned to righteous.

A Steep Price

Paul presses on to elaborate how God justifies the sinner and how this declaration of justification is received. He writes, "God presented Christ as a sacrifice of atonement, through the shedding of his blood—to be received by faith" (Rom. 3:25a). Notice, first, that Paul mentions how God justifies the sinner: Jesus was presented "as a sacrifice of atonement."[7]

This atoning sacrifice is the appeasement of God's wrath (satisfying his justice) and the expiation (removal) of our guilt. Unfortunately, all too often, God is presented as a heavenly Santa Clause. Such is not the case. God is loving, merciful, and gracious, but he is also just, holy, and righteous. God presents a picture of this atoning sacrifice in the Book of Leviticus while describing the

---

[6]Paul refers both to the process of being holy in Christ (positional sanctification) and growing in holiness in this life (progressive sanctification). The next chapter will deal with the idea of progressive sanctification.

[7]The phrase "sacrifice of atonement" comes from the Greek word "ἱλαστήριον" (hilasterion) and is translated as "propitiation" in some English translations.

requirements for the Day of Atonement (Lev. 16:8-10). He told Aaron to take two goats and cast lots. One goat was sacrificed. The other goat was prayed over and sent into the wilderness, carrying away the sins of the people. This ceremony was performed as a living picture of atonement in which sins were both paid for and removed. Justice was satisfied while the condemned was forgiven and restored.

Jesus' work on the cross is the ultimate fulfillment of the actions performed on both goats. The Day of Atonement is one of many events foreshadowing of the coming of Jesus found in the Old Testament. Through Jesus' death on the cross and resurrection, the wrath of God toward sin is satisfied because the penalty of sin is dealt with justly. Moreover, through Jesus' death and resurrection, the believer's guilt is removed because the penalty for sin is gone and forgiveness extended.

An important note to make at this point is that such redemption is freely offered and freely received, but those facts do not mean it is free. A cost occurred in the purchase of our redemption. How can God be both just and merciful? If God merely overlooks sin as a result of his mercy, he is an unjust judge. If God exercises his justice without mercy, we are doomed, and he can't claim to be compassionate. So, God maintains his justice in condemning and judging sin while extending mercy by taking our place and paying our penalty for sin. In doing so, both the guilt and consequence of sin are gone, and the wrath of God is satisfied.

Secondly, Paul explains how this benefit of justification through Christ's redemptive work is received. It is "to be received by faith" (Citation?). Since faith was discussed somewhat in the last chapter, a brief illustration will be provided here to show how active faith is necessary to receive the benefit of redemption. Imagine you received a letter that a long lost loved one who had passed away, that you had inherited one million dollars, and that the money was waiting for you at the courthouse. Is the money yours? Well, maybe in the sense that it is a provisional promise that has been extended to you, but it is not yours in actuality until you receive it by going and getting it. You have to believe the money is there, decide to go get it, and then accept it.

Why is Jesus necessary for our substitutionary sacrifice before God?

In Romans 3:25b–26, Paul expands his point and provided three reasons to support God's justifying work through Jesus Christ.[8] He writes, "He did this to demonstrate his righteousness, because in his forbearance he had left the sins committed beforehand unpunished—he did it to demonstrate his righteousness at the present time, so as to be just and the one who justifies those who have faith in Jesus."

First, God's justifying work through the death of Jesus Christ *revealed God's righteousness in dealing with past sin.* "Paul's meaning is rather that God 'postponed' the full penalty due sins in the Old Covenant, allowing sinners to stand before him without their having provided an adequate 'satisfaction' of the demands of his holy justice (cf. Heb. 10:4)."[9] In other words, sins committed by humanity before Jesus came were not overlooked. God, in his justice, did not dismiss the sin debt previously accumulated; rather, he merely delayed full judgment until the cross. God did not compromise his justice and holiness in extending mercy to mankind.[10]

Secondly, God's justifying work through the death of Jesus Christ *showed his righteousness in dealing with present sin.* Jesus' substitutionary sacrifice was sufficient, not only for past sin but also for present and future sin. These first two points reiterate the same basic underlying principle: God does not overlook sin but deals with all sin justly for all time. No sin, in any age, is merely dismissed. A penalty must be paid. A consequence is demanded for a violation of God's holy law. For God to dismiss sin outright would make God unjust. Since God is just, he dealt with sin through the cross.

---

[8] Thomas R. Schreiner, *Romans*, (Grand Rapids: Baker, 1998), 195.

[9] Douglas Moo, *The Epistle to the Romans*, NICNT (Grand Rapids: Eerdmans, 1996), 240.

[10] Schreiner, 196.

Thirdly, God's justifying work through the death of Jesus Christ *showed that he is just and the sole justifier of anyone who places their faith in Christ.* This reason clarifies and punctuates all that Paul declared in verses 25 and 26. Not only was previous sin atoned for in the cross of Jesus Christ, but present sin was atoned for from the time of the cross until the end of the age when Jesus returns. Therefore, those who place their faith in Jesus as the one who stood in their place in judgment on the cross bearing their penalty for sin are justified before God. Their sins have been atoned once for all. Notice, again, that the text emphasizes that only God can justify someone's sins, and it is only through the atoning work of Jesus Christ that justification can be experienced.

What Now?

What grace and mercy! God did what we could not do for ourselves. He paid for our sin. He provided atonement and a means to be justified before him, a holy God, without compromising his character. As a result, we have no ground for boasting before God (Rom. 3:27). We do not come before God offering him a sacrifice of good works. We do not claim any righteousness of our own; rather, we revel in the work of the cross and boast in the glory of a crucified and risen Savior, the Lord Jesus Christ. God in his infinite grace made provision for us.

God has dealt with sin on our behalf. The reality is that...

.... *we are all guilty.*

.... *our guilt demands punishment.*

...*Jesus bore the punishment we deserved on the cross.*

.... *anyone who trusts in Jesus is justified (made right) before God.*

For the believer in Christ, your status has been changed from condemned to righteous. No matter how dirty your past is, God made provision in Christ. What a beautiful truth. So, my friend, can I offer some advice?

Stop living in guilt over past sin. Several years ago, my wife and I had the privilege of ministering to a brokenhearted lady. Natalie[11] would come into my office on occasion weeping. She would always say the same thing, "You just don't know what I've done," and I would always respond the same, "Regardless, God does, and his grace is sufficient." She would say, "You don't understand my past," and I would say, "Dear one, you don't understand grace." She was paralyzed by this idea that somehow her sin was too bad, too horrible, to be atoned for by Jesus. If you are currently struggling with sin, repent and look to the cross. Read Psalm 103, and rejoice in your salvation. Confess your sin, and trust in a forgiving, reconciling, justifying God. Your sin is why you need the cross. Then again, maybe it is not your current sin binding your heart and conscience to the anvil of guilt but is your past. Maybe, like Natalie, you are overwhelmed by your failures. Maybe you stumbled across an old yearbook, and memories flood back, triggering these emotions. Maybe these feelings were triggered from a Facebook photo of an ill-advised night out or an old song on the radio. When the enemy starts to whisper in your ear, fight him with God's truth. Defend yourself based on God's work and not that of your own doing. If you are in Christ, those mistakes no longer define you. You are righteous in Christ. Allow your failure to drive you to embrace, cherish, and love the cross more. Allow your failure to help you drink deeply from the well of forgiveness and feast at the table of mercy. God is greater than your sin (Rom. 5:20–21). If God has forgiven you, who are you to dishonor Christ's sacrifice on your behalf and seek to embrace for yourself the punishment that he bore for you? Remember, Jesus cried out, "It is finished!" (John 19:30)

My father-in-law passed away suddenly in 2008. It's hard to describe what it is like to receive "that" phone call. Shock, numbness, and then sadness bombarded my mind. He was a great man, and we were heartbroken. I was a student in seminary, and we were living in Indiana at the time. I went home, got my wife and children, then we headed off to Alabama for the funeral. As great as my father-in-

---

[11] Throughout the book, personal names and genders have been changed.

law was, he did have one flaw. He was a bit of a paperwork hoarder. As a matter of fact, he had every mobile phone bill he had ever received in paper trash bags under his bed. In an effort to help my mother-in-law, I volunteered to go through and organize all of the paperwork. In one of the files, I came across a bill that was not that old. It was a loan he had taken out for a reasonable amount of money at an unreasonable interest rate of over twenty percent. My heart sank. I panicked, imagining how the bill had grown over the last few months. Nervously, I called to inquire about the bill. I gave them the account number, and the lady responded, "Thanks for calling, Mr. McClendon. That account has been paid in full." Oh, was I relieved! What beautiful words, "paid in full!" For all those of us who have placed our faith in Christ, the Bible reveals that, as a result of Jesus' atoning work, we have been justified by God, and our sins have been "paid in full." No unpaid balance is left on our sin debt.

Commit to live out the righteousness that is yours in Christ Jesus. More on this topic will be discussed in the next chapter, but if God has made you righteous, if you have been freed from the bondage of sin, and if you are empowered by the Spirit of Christ, then live righteously to the glory of God. You can live for him. Your status has been changed. Your position before his throne has been altered. Your destiny is fixed. You can live for him as his child to his glory.

Envision the possibility. Envision how different our homes, our communities, and our churches would be if we lived out the reality of this new status that is ours in Christ Jesus. What if the fact that we are made right with God through Jesus Christ defined us, not the small slights we receive from colleagues, friends, and family? Think about how much different our responses to those people would be as we lived freely for Jesus and free from performance-driven slavery. What a difference it would make in our lives and the lives of those around us. When we truly believe that we are only made right with God through Jesus Christ, it makes a world of difference. When this truth captures our heart, we become more and more apt to tell others about his amazing grace, we become more apt to trust fully in Jesus, and we become more apt to live fully for him.

Remember, we can't snowball God. Let's stop trying to convince ourselves that we are good on our own standing and instead embrace the truth that our righteousness comes from Christ alone and his work on the cross.

Not What My Hands Have Done

Not what my hands have done
can save my guilty soul;
Not what my toiling flesh has borne
can make my spirit whole.
Not what I feel or do
can give me peace with God;
Not all my prayers and sighs and tears
can bear my awful load.

Your voice alone, O Lord,
can speak to me of grace;
Your power alone, O Son of God,
can all my sin erase.
No other work but Yours,
no other blood will do;
No strength but that which is divine
can bear me safely through.

Thy work alone, O Christ,
can ease this weight of sin;
Thy blood alone, O Lamb of God,
can give me peace within.
Thy love to me, O God,
not mine, O Lord, to Thee,
Can rid me of this dark unrest,
And set my spirit free.

I bless the Christ of God;
I rest on love divine;
And with unfaltering lip and heart
I call this Savior mine.
His cross dispels each doubt;
I bury in His tomb
Each thought of unbelief and fear,
each lingering shade of gloom.

> *I praise the God of grace;*
> *I trust His truth and might;*
> *He calls me His, I call Him mine,*
> *My God, my joy and light.*
> *'Tis He Who saveth me,*
> *and freely pardon gives;*
> *I love because He loveth me,*
> *I live because He lives.*[12]

Questions for Reflection:

1 Have you ever tried to justify your sin? What excuses do we sometimes use to make our sin seem insignificant?

2 After reading the chapter, how would you describe justification? What does it mean to be justified before God?

3 Why couldn't God simply ignore our sin? If he ignored sin, how would this change our view of God?

4 Is there a past sin that continues to consume you? Why does this sin have such a hold?

5 How do we learn to live in the forgiveness of Jesus? What daily practices might help you constantly remember what Christ had done for you?

---

[12]Horatius Bonar, *Not What These Hands Have Done*, 1861.

CHAPTER 3
EXPECTATION: HOLINESS BEFORE GOD

The Boring Basics

It was a beautiful fall Saturday in Missouri, and that means college football in our (Adam's) home. Okay, it means college football and kids soccer, at least at this point in my children's lives. Knowing our afternoon would be taken up with errands and activities, I called all the kids into the living room around 9 a.m. I asked them to sit down, very officially. After turning off the television, I turned to them and, in a serious tone, said, "I have an important job for you to do." They sat up a little straighter, waiting with great anticipation. "What would Dad want us to do?" they wondered. "Maybe build an addition onto the house? Maybe go and start a new business venture? Maybe go hunting for hidden treasure." I mean, after all, you know how the minds of young children work. I declared in a manly voice, "I need you to clean the house!" You can imagine what kind of response that brought. "Uhhhh, Daaad!" What was the problem? They don't like cleaning the house! Who does? They wanted to do something more spectacular than cleaning up around their own home.

Like my children, we don't like to do the basics. The ordinary bores us. We want to do "glamorous" things. We want the tasks that seem important or fun to us, and in doing so, we sometimes dismiss the tasks that are mundane, even though many of them are the most important things to do in life! My children often want to work with me. For example, they might come in, see me hanging a picture, and say, "I want to help." The problem is they grab stuff that is not helpful at the time, like a saw. When this happens, they get a lecture.

37

"If you want to help, you have to help in a way that is, well, helpful. In other words, you have to follow my lead. I know you want to do things you think are fun, but I don't need you to use the saw right now. I need you to hold the tape measure so I can mark the wall."

We can act a lot like children in our spiritual lives sometimes. We can get so caught up in trying to serve God that we forget who God wants us to be and the basic things God has asked us to do. In doing so, we forget to be faithful in the little stuff. For example:

handwritten margin note: Makes me think of the word hypocritical

- ❖ We can work hard on Thursday to prepare a Sunday school lesson on patience and kindness then cut people off and scream in frustration during our Friday morning commute.

- ❖ We can listen to a coworker struggling with life and counsel them about trusting God then come home and stress over bills that came in the mail.

- ❖ We can post religious pictures on social media then later surf the Internet for websites we shouldn't view.

- ❖ We can smile at church as a greeter then be disrespectful to the single mother waitressing because she messed up our Sunday lunch order.

- ❖ We can make sure we look nice for church then talk about other people behind their backs or pass judgment on those who aren't like us.

The last two chapters addressed how God in his infinite mercy made a way for us to be in a right standing before him through faith in Jesus Christ. Well, what now? "I'm saved from the judgment my sin deserved, but what's next? Do I just live my life?"

Not only has God saved us for a new life in heaven as Christians, but he has also provided a new orientation for our lives here on earth. God not only declared us righteous, but he also provided a way by the presence of his Spirit for us to live out the righteousness that is ours. That is in part why Jesus said believers are born again. We as believers have a new calling on our lives to reflect the nature of the incredible God who saved us in the midst of this broken world. Moreover, God not only called us to live a holy life, but he also provided us with the ability to live a holy life through the renewing presence of the Holy Spirit, who now resides within us. Thus, part of being the people of God is to be holy. So, let's look at just one way this idea is developed in the Scriptures.

A New Direction

Peter, before meeting Jesus, spent his days casting fishing nets. Not a bad gig. I know a lot of people who would love to be out of the cubicle and on the lake every day, but Peter's life had no meaning until he met Jesus. Everything changed after his encounter with the Messiah. He eventually became an apostle of Jesus Christ and a key leader in the church. After Jesus ascended, Peter spent his life leading and encouraging fellow Christians. He begins his first letter by reminding us of the awe-inspiring salvation that is ours through Jesus.

> *"Praise be to the God and Father of our Lord Jesus Christ! In his great mercy he has given us new birth into a living hope through the resurrection of Jesus Christ from the dead, and into an inheritance that can never perish, spoil or fade. This inheritance is kept in heaven for you, who through faith are shielded by God's power until the coming of the salvation that is ready to be revealed in the last time."*

1 Pet. 1:3–5

God "has given us" a new life, a new hope, through Jesus. Even in this present life, we now have an inheritance that can never be taken away. We have a spectacular future that is protected for us by the very power of God. Believers in Jesus have a heavenly destination purchased and secured. Despite the difficulties of life's journey, our future is guaranteed. Nevertheless, Peter didn't stop there. He didn't just cast this grand view of heaven and have us wallow in the brokenness of this world in anticipation of something more. Rather, Peter revealed to us that God has an expectation for our lives here and now while we treasure the promise of our glorious future. God has a goal for us to live in light of this heavenly hope in a way that will reflect his nature to others and draw more people into the kingdom that is promised for all who trust in Jesus. Peter puts it this way:

> *"Therefore, preparing your minds for action, and being sober-minded, set your hope fully on the grace that will be brought to you at the revelation of Jesus Christ. As obedient children, do not be conformed to the passions of your former ignorance, but as he who called you is holy, you also be holy in all you conduct, since it is written, 'You shall be holy, for I am holy.'"*

1 Pet. 1:13–16[13]

So, let's walk through this passage together.

"Therefore," in light of the amazing salvation that is yours in Jesus (1:1-9), in light of a salvation so amazing it piques the curiosity of angelic realm (1:12), "prepare your minds for action, and being sober-minded, set your hope fully on the grace that will be brought to you at the revelation of Jesus Christ" (1:13). As believers, we do not find our hope in this world; instead, our hope is in the coming of King Jesus, who bring us into an eternal heavenly kingdom where there will be no more death, pain, or sorrow (1 Cor. 15:54-55; Rev 21:4). How do we set our hope on the coming of Jesus? Peter tells us that we do so "by preparing our minds for action, and being self-controlled in our thinking (sober-minded)."[14] Peter emphasizes the reality that our minds need to be disciplined to stay focused on the endgame of Jesus' return as we endure the curse-filled shrapnel of this world.

---

[13] *ESV* is cited here instead of the *NIV*. The *NIV* translates the beginning of verse 13 as "with minds that are alert." This translation is good, but the *ESV* translates the passage in a way that seems to capture the emphasis of the Greek language a little more clearly. The *ESV* specifically states that we are to "prepare our minds for action." The emphasis on action communicates the first century idea of "girding up one's loins" better than simple "alertness." The rest of the chapter will utilize the *NIV*.

[14] Thomas R. Schreiner, *1 Peter*, NAC (Nashville: B&H, 2003), 78.

The idea of "preparing our minds for action," comes from a Greek idiom.[15] The literal translation is "to gird up the loins of your mind." Now, "girding up one's loins" was something done when preparing for battle, running, or hard work. People in biblical times wore clothing, robes and tunics and such, that would flow around both legs at once. The image is similar to what you would envision in a modern day full-length skirt. This design made it difficult to move fast or run, so the people of that day would "gird up their loins." To "gird up their loins" means they would reach down like they were going to touch the ground in front of them. While remaining bent, they would reach and grab the backmost portion of the fabric closest to the ground and pull it forward. Then, standing, they would tuck it into their belt. Doing so resulted in makeshift pants allowing them a much better range of motion and securing any loose fabric that could impede movement. In light of that background, Peter literally told us to get our minds ready for intense action and not allow our thinking to become dull. We have to remain mentally focused on the inheritance that awaits all those who are faithful in Christ Jesus.

The emphasis here, and throughout Scripture, on the necessity of remaining mentally vigilant is one reason why the church has historically (and rightly) encouraged daily Bible reading and the memorization of Scripture. Yet, it seems in today's society that a misunderstanding exists concerning the purpose of spending time in the Bible. We do not simply read the Bible for information and then check it off our list to go and live our lives. The goal of taking in the Bible is not for information only but rather to engage the truths of the Bible for the purpose of applying those truths to our mind and our lives. It is reading the Bible for the purpose of thinking and living more transformed into the image of Jesus (Rom. 12:1–2). Attentive Bible reading and memorization provides a framework of thinking whereby we are able to discipline our minds to conform to

---

[15]Johannes P. Louw and Eugene Albert Nida, *Greek-English Lexicon of the New Testament: Based on Semantic Domains* (New York: United Bible Societies, 1996), 332.

the thinking, ways, and will of God. This idea of training our mind by God's word is repeatedly emphasized in the Old and New Testaments of the Bible.

> *"Keep this Book of the Law always on your lips; meditate on it day and night, so that you may be careful to do everything written in it. Then you will be prosperous and successful."*

> Joshua 1:8

> *"I have hidden your word in my heart that I might not sin against you."*

> Psalm 119:11

> *"Do not conform to the pattern of this world, but be transformed by the renewing of your mind. Then you will be able to test and approve what God's will is—his good, pleasing and perfect will."*

> Romans 12:2

> *"You were taught, with regard to your former way of life, to put off your old self, which is being corrupted by its deceitful desires; to be made new in the attitude of your minds."*

> Ephesians 4:22–23

Unfortunately, all too often we lose the mental battle early. We fail to prepare our minds for spiritual, mental, and emotional challenges. We have little motivation to take the time to mentally engage the truths of God until we find ourselves neck deep in despair, sin, shame, and brokenness. Think about the irony here. We do not engage the godly truths designed to protect us from and preserve us through the evil of this world until we've already fallen victim to the evil of this world. We naturally understand that, to be effective in a fight, we must have trained for that fight beforehand, not in the aftermath of it. Let us think of it this way. Take MMA (mixed martial arts) as an example. Could you imagine a fighter knowing a title fight is coming up soon and thinking, "I hope I do well" and just going through the motions of life? No way! He would get destroyed. What sense would it make if, after getting demolished in the ring, the fighter said, "Well, I obviously need to work on some things," and then he or she goes into strict training after the fight for only a month before falling back into old routines? That is not a recipe for success. Fighters train before the fight, not just in the aftermath of it. Yet, so many of us as believers go through our normal routines in life and then find ourselves in personal and spiritual conflict, not mentally prepared for the borage of questions, temptations, and turmoil that fills our mind. We then, in reaction to our crisis, cry out to God. We find ourselves spending time in the Bible and meditating on truths, just to end up a few months down the road drifting back into the same routines that left us unprepared for the difficulty we recently experienced.

Instead of such an ineffective approach, we are called to train our minds consistently to stay focused on the pending grace and glory we will experience when we meet Jesus at the end of the age. We are to train our minds not to get distracted by the petty and temporal glamour of this world. We are to train our minds to not lose hope due to the chaos, evil, and brokenness of our present circumstances.

Furthermore, as we focus on the glory to come, we are called to be motivated to live differently in our current circumstances. We are called to live in a manner that is in some way distinct from the world and our former lives because of the hope we have in Jesus. Sadly, all too often it seems that we are not motivated to live differently given the hope Jesus brings; rather, we are often motivated by a worldly focus.

❖ We take the trash out, not because we seek to show our spouse love and honor but to stop the nagging.

❖ We stop wasting time at work and knock out the overdue project, not because we are called to be faithful employees working for the glory of God, but to silence an overbearing boss.

❖ We seek to lose weight, not because we are seeking to be a good steward of the body God has given us so that we might live longer to influence our neighborhood and the nations for the cause of Christ but to be more attractive to others.

Peter throughout this section revealed that God commands to live differently in light of the hope we have in Jesus. God sets a clear expectation for us as we await the return of Christ: holiness.

Pushing Back and Stepping Up

Peter presents this expectation in two ways. He shows what we are not to do first, followed by what we *are* to do. In so doing, he states the same expectation from two perspectives lest we miss his point. He commands us first, "As obedient children, do not conform to the evil desires you had when you lived in ignorance" (1 Pet. 1:14). We are to stop being conformed to the passions (or lusts) that were ours in ignorance (in other words, before we knew the wonder of Jesus).

Now, as an aside, if you are still reading this book and you have not surrendered your life to Jesus, you are living for a lesser love. You are living in spiritual ignorance. Please know that Jesus has something so much better for you. Jesus has a plan for your life and a personal expectation for you to live a holy life for his glory. This new life begins when you trust in Jesus as the one who paid for your sins on the cross and you surrender your life to him.

For those who have experienced this transformational grace Jesus offers, Peter instructs us to stop living according to our sinful desires. We are not to give in. We are not to succumb to the tempting pressures of this world. When I was a child, I loved Play-Doh. (Okay, maybe I still do, but don't tell anyone.) Play-Doh is some of the coolest stuff ever. I remember when Play-Doh came out with a new tool where you could place an attachment on the front of this small press and squeeze out the Play-Doh into various shapes. The Play-Doh would go in the contraption as a lump and come out squeezed into a precise mold. That is what Peter told us to watch out for. We need to fix our minds on the future return of our king and not allow ourselves to "conform" (i.e. succumb, be molded) to sinful desires, specifically those that controlled our life before trusting Jesus. Don't let sinful desires pressure you into rebelling against your savior. Don't continue in your sinful pre-Christian pattern.

- ❖ Before Jesus, you dressed provocatively seeking attention. Stop! Don't give in! Dress modestly, and seek to have your behavior highlight the transformational greatness of God.

- ❖ Before Jesus, you swore and told dirty jokes. No more! Stop! Use your words to build up people and to point them to faith in Christ.

- ❖ Before Jesus, you had bursts of anger and were argumentative. Stop! Seek to be at peace with others living in a way that shows your hope is not in things working out here but in Jesus working them out when he returns.

- ❖ Before Jesus, you thought it was pleasurable to look at illicit images, believing it gave you a sense of power and significance. Stop! These are people made in the image of God. Trust in God to satisfy you, and find sexual fulfillment in accordance with his holy and acceptable design.

I heard this saying long ago, "If you don't want to fall down, don't walk on a slippery floor." We need to be people who avoid sin, in part, by avoiding sinful situations.

- ❖ Struggle with sleeping around and drinking? Stop going to bars and parties. Stop going on dates by yourself.

- ❖ Struggle with envy? Stop surfing shopping and social media sites.

- ❖ Struggling with addictions? Pour the booze and pills in the toilet.

- ❖ Struggling with racism? Burn all of your symbols and the materials you own, which promote racism in your heart.

❖ Struggling with addiction to "Scratch Off" lottery tickets? Pay at the pump only, and don't go into the stores.

❖ Struggling with the time you're wasting playing video games? Sell your gaming system.

❖ Struggling with elicit websites? Put the computer in the most public place in the house, and if you live alone, sell your computer.

This idea of avoiding temptation is encouraged in part of the Lord's Prayer as we cry out to God for help, "And lead us not into temptation but deliver us from the evil one" (Matt. 6:13).

We have a new orientation in Jesus and a new expectation for our lives: holiness. Instead of allowing ourselves to be pressured into the past sinful ignorant mold we lived in before we met Jesus, we are commanded to trade in all those old passions for new ones. We are instructed to be conformed by a new mold, a mold that is fashioned after the character of the God we serve—which reflects his holy nature. That is the other side of the equation Peter presents. "But just as he who called you is holy, so be holy in all you do; for it is written: 'Be holy, because I am holy'" (1 Pet. 1:15–16).

The Christian life is not passive. God expects something of us and has enabled us by his Spirit to live the life to which he has called us. He has given us a precious purchased life. I often fall into the trap of thinking that salvation was free. My salvation wasn't free. It was freely offered to me, but it was purchased at a very high price. I read this story a while back and felt it highlighted how understanding the high price paid for my new life can change my perspective. Karen Morerod went shopping at a store looking for a sweater. Like all of us, she wanted to find one at the best price possible, so she "went to the clearance rack to start looking."[16] She continues describing what happened next,

---

[16] Karen Morerod, "Lessons Learned from a Sweater: The Value of God's Gift of Grace," *Decision* (1999), 39.

As I flipped through the sweaters, one caught my eye. It was the right color and the right size, and best of all, the price tag was marked $8.00. Without much thought, I made my purchase.

At home I slipped on the sweater. Its texture was like silk. I had made my purchase so quickly that I hadn't noticed how smooth and elegant the sweater was. Then I saw the original price tag: $124.00!

I gasped. I had never owned any clothing of that value. I had come home with what I thought was a 'cheap buy,' but the original price was quite high. I had been oblivious to its value.[17]

Later she remarks, "Just as I had with my sweater, I often treated Jesus' blood like a 'cheap purchase'...but I was forgetting about the great price that Jesus paid so that God could forgive my sins. His grace, though free to me, carried a high price tag—the life of His very own Son."[18]

For us who are believers in Christ, we are called to live in a manner that reflects the holy nature of God in light of the amazing grace we have been given now and will experience in full at Christ's return. We are expected to reflect the holiness of God in our attitudes and actions as a result of the righteousness that is ours through Jesus. God expects us to be a holy people.

Things to Consider

Living a holy life in obedience to God is his desire for us as we anticipate the return of King Jesus. What we do reflects to some degree what we actually believe about God, but even beyond that, what we do matters to God. Take time now to reflect upon your life, the actions of this past week. What do these actions tell you about your faith? What sins were you serving? Were you serving sins in

[17]Ibid.
[18]Ibid.

the pursuit of pleasure, power, security, wealth, self? The point isn't to add guilt or shame upon our life but to help us see where we have bought into treasuring the sins of the world. The point is to help us see where we have forgotten the beautiful truth that God saved us to free us from these sins so that we could walk in holiness. As you reflect upon this past week, confess any area of your life where you see you were living for something less than to reflect the holiness of God for the glory of God. God is gracious and has already forgiven you in Jesus for all sin: past, present, and future. You are redeemed by the blood of the Lamb; however, you still need to acknowledge the impact sin makes on your immediate intimacy with God and your effectiveness in reflecting the nature of God to a lost world. You also need to remember that grace is extended in part to free you from every day sinful patterns and enable you to walk in holiness (Rom. 6).

Beginning today, if you are a believer in Jesus, there are three truths I want to challenge you to memorize and embrace. Maybe you need to say them out loud, write them on a note and place it on your bathroom mirror to remind you, or place a notification on your phone to pop up daily for a week. Whatever it takes, begin to memorize and embrace these three intermingled truths. Here they are:

First, **"I can walk in holiness!"** Do you know the story of *The Little Engine That Could*? He chugged and he chugged up that mountain full of self-determination, uttering, "I think I can! I think I can!" He reached down deep and found the strength to not give up and push through the impossible. That is not what the Bible teaches you to do. Your life before Jesus was a mess, and despite all the determination in the world, you could not live up to the holiness of God because of your sin. Rather, God calls you not to a life of self-determination but to a life of self-surrender to his Spirit. When you gave your life to Jesus, he filled you with his Spirit. The same spiritual power that raised Jesus from the dead, that very same resurrection and death-defying power, now lives in you (Rom. 8:11). You are now called to trust in him, submit to him, and obey him.

Galatians 5:16 declares, "So I say, walk by the Spirit, and you will not gratify the desires of the flesh." Thus, when confronted with temptation and doubt, utter, "He will empower me! He will empower me!" Place your confidence for obedience not in yourself but in God's Spirit.

Second, **"I don't have to sin!"** Sin is a choice. Whether you are sinning by doing what God has forbidden or you are sinning by not doing what God has commanded, you do not have to sin. Sin is a choice. As just mentioned above, God's Holy Spirit now lives in you. Realize that sin is not a defaulted position for the believer; it's a choice. Quit choosing sin over righteousness. You'll be amazed what this subtle shift of mental preparedness will do in your life.

Third, **"God expects me to be holy!"** This point was repeatedly demonstrated in the earlier parts of this chapter. The question is, "Do you believe it yet?" Do you accept that God not only "wants" but "expects" holiness in your life? God wants to bless you with the gift of experiential, everyday, walking-in-grace holiness! Yes, you are holy positionally in Christ. Yes, you are called holy because of Jesus' sacrifice on your behalf. Now, God wants you to live out the holiness that is yours eternally in Christ in your daily walk with him. He wants you to live for him before a world that desperately needs to know him. God wants you to experience the power of the Kingdom of Heaven as he works through you to conquer the power of sin and death in your daily existence. When you walk in victory in this life, you are giving a glimpse to the world of the ultimate victory that will come when Jesus returns.[19]

History reveals that, while in Oxford, Charles Wesley was a part of a group devoted to studying the Bible and growing in holiness. This group became known, among other things, as The Holy Club.[20]

---

[19]This picture of the presence of the God's powerful kingdom in this world is demonstrated through Jesus as a sign for the physical and spiritual world throughout the Gospels.

[20] A good summary of the history is provided at http://wesley.nnu.edu/john-wesley/john-wesley-the-methodist/chapter-v-

John Wesley later became the effective leader of this group. Together, he and his brother Charles were committed to leading the group in consecrating themselves more and more fully to God. In examining their lives, the group continually developed questions. Among those sets of questions was a set of twenty-two questions they would ask in order to hold themselves accountable and allow for self-reflection. These questions are still a great tool for the soul seeking to look for areas in which to grow in holiness, and they commonly occur in this form:[21]

1. Am I consciously or unconsciously creating the impression that I am better than I really am? In other words, am I a hypocrite?
2. Am I honest in all my acts and words, or do I exaggerate?
3. Do I confidentially pass on to another what was told to me in confidence?
4. Can I be trusted?
5. Am I a slave to dress, friends, work, or habits?
6. Am I self-conscious, self-pitying, or self-justifying?
7. Did the Bible live in me today?
8. Do I give it time to speak to me every day?
9. Am I enjoying prayer?
10. When did I last speak to someone else about my faith?
11. Do I pray about the money I spend?
12. Do I get to bed on time and get up on time?

---

the-holy-club/. For a more detailed account of the clubs beginnings and early years, read Martin Schmidt, *John Wesley: A Theological Biography: From 17th June 1703 until 24th May 1738*, vol. 1, trans. Norman P. Goldhawk (Eugene: Wipf and Stock, 2016), 96–103.

[21]Questions such as these are frequently used by the Wesley's and appear in different forms. An example can be seen in Frank Whaling, ed., *John and Charles Wesley: Selected Prayers, Hymns, Journal Notes, Sermons, Letters, and Treaties* (New York: Paulist Press, 1981), 85–87. The twenty-two questions that follow in this chapter are what most frequently appear in publications and websites today as an example of the "Holy Club" checklist and valuable for the purposes presented here.

13. Do I disobey God in anything?
14. Do I insist upon doing something about which my conscience is uneasy?
15. Am I defeated in any part of my life?
16. Am I jealous, impure, critical, irritable, touchy, or distrustful?
17. How do I spend my spare time?
18. Am I proud?
19. Do I thank God that I am not as other people, especially as the Pharisees, who despised the publican?
20. Is there anyone whom I fear, dislike, disown, criticize, hold a resentment toward or disregard? If so, what am I doing about it?
21. Do I grumble or complain constantly?
22. Is Christ real to me?

Take some time in the next couple of weeks to go over these questions and examine your life before the Lord.

Remember the story of my kids earlier? Remember me gathering them together to talk? They anticipated instructions to do something spectacular and what they received was a challenge to do the mundane. Faithfulness in the mundane, moment-by-moment, grind of life is spectacular. That is what God wants and expects from us. Let us live holy lives even in the midst of the most mundane moments.

What if we took God's expectation of holiness seriously? What if we believed that we were expected to be holy and we were capable in Christ of living a holy life? What if we lived in light of the fact that one day Jesus will return and expects to find us holy? What difference would that make in our personal testimonies at home, work, and even church? Wouldn't that begin to diffuse the accurate accusation the world makes saying that the church is full of hypocrites? How can we expect the blessings of God in our personal and church lives when we fail to strive to live holy in accordance with his most basic commands? And isn't it possible that, the more we live out holy obedience to God in the most mundane areas of everyday life, just maybe we could also be transforming into instruments through which God may do something spectacular? Remember MMA fighters, the ones who win the big fights, are those who have done the necessary conditioning and training before the fight, not afterward.

Just think of the impact that living a holy life for the glory of God would make. Think of the peace it would bring. And, if you are not a believer in Christ, you will never understand this level of peace until you surrender to him. I implore you to turn your life over to Jesus today. He wants to equip you to live the life he has for you, a holy and good life.

Questions for Reflection

How would you define holiness? What does it mean to be holy?

How does the promise of Christ's return empower our holiness? What role does the Holy Spirit play in making us holy?

Are there aspects of your thinking that inhibit your pursuit of holiness? How can you "gird your mind" against these?

Are there any sinful situations that you need to avoid in order to pursue holiness?

Which of Wesley's questions do you find most challenging? Why?

How has this chapter challenged or affirmed your understanding of life as a Christian?

CHAPTER 4
MOTIVATION: GLORY OF GOD

Bad Fuel

I (Adam) was sent overseas for my final year in the military four months after we got married. My wife stuck it out in North Carolina for a while, but after two hurricanes, each of which flooded our apartment, we decided it would be best if she moved back to Alabama, where we were from. A few months later, I was honorably discharged and joined her. One night, shortly after arriving back home, I had to go to my mother's house to pick up some furniture. My in-laws let me borrow their Chevy Suburban to haul it back. After picking up the furniture and heading home, I realized the Suburban was low on fuel, so I stopped at a gas station. (Now, at this point, I want to preface the rest of the story. I was a twenty-one-year-old with limited to no mechanical ability, who didn't know how to change oil, windshield wiper blades, or anything else, and I certainly didn't know the difference between a regular and diesel engine.) As I stepped out to fill up, I looked at the pumps and noticed the option of diesel. I knew my father-in-law had one vehicle that ran on diesel, but I had never bothered to ask which one, nor had I really cared before this moment. Did this vehicle take regular or diesel fuel? I didn't know. I stood there trying to figure it out, but I was lost. Finally, I dug out some change and called them from a pay phone. (Yes, I'm that old. Mobile phones were not prevalent, and pay phones were still on every corner.) One problem. They were not home, and I had to get going. So, I left them a message that sounded something like this, "Um, I'm at a gas station. The Suburban needs gas, and I don't know if it takes regular or diesel fuel. If you are there, please pick up. Um, I guess you aren't home, so I'll just have to guess." I hung up. Thankfully, I guessed right. When I arrived back at my in-law's house and walked in the door, my father-n-law was standing in the kitchen. He looked at me and without hesitation said, "Are you stupid? How do you not know the difference between regular and diesel fuel?" Needless to say, his generation didn't go through sensitivity training, and I lost a little manly credibility with my father-n-law that day. I responded, "Why? What's the big deal? What would have happened if I had used the wrong fuel?" At this point, I began to get my educational lecture on how different fuels can make or break an engine.

Just like a physical engine, the fuel we use for our spiritual tank matters. That which we turn to in order to fuel, motivate, and drive our spiritual lives has a tremendous impact on us. Some of us are using the wrong fuel and wondering why we feel like we are clunking along in life. Much of the first half of my life was lived for myself. I wanted to be famous, I wanted to matter, and I wanted to be viewed as a man. Those motivations led to some horrible decisions. For example, I was working at Southeastern Bible College in Birmingham Alabama in 2003, when one of the college students with whom I was a friend invited me to go hiking and hanging out with some guys for his birthday at Little River Canyon Falls. We arrived, and it was gorgeous. Only one problem—we were supposed to go swimming in a nice, calm, cool pool at the base of a waterfall, but it had rained the day before. The water was way up from its normal level, which resulted in a fast-flowing rapid. We walked to the top of the falls, and the water was rushing over the edge. I asked if anyone was going out on the falls. Everyone looked at me like I was crazy. I said, "Come on, guys. It's no big deal." Part of me foolishly believed this, but the greater part of me just wanted to be cool and do something that no one else was willing to do. I continued to prod and then boasted, "Well, I'm going out there." As I waded out onto the falls, I quickly realized I was in trouble. It was taking all of my strength not to get pulled over the edge. I ended up about twenty feet from shore at the edge of the falls on a rock about forty feet up from the pool below. I was stuck. I couldn't get back. I was slipping due to the pressure of the water that was still hitting me. Jumping from this location could mean hitting some rocks, and if that happened, I would certainly drown in the rapids as they swept me downstream. I didn't want to ask for help and tried to look calm but eventually lost the façade and admitted I was in trouble. They had to make a human chain to rescue me, all because I was driven to try and impress others. I can't tell you how many times before or since I've gotten into trouble because I was motivated by a desire to look good, be popular, be a man, and impress others. The drive for self-glorification is bad fuel and results in a life that is lived for lesser glory.

What about you? What fuels your life? Is it the promotion of self in the pursuit of fame or success? That fuel has led many a young ladies to pose provocatively beyond comfort zones and the boundaries of modesty, resulting in regret. That fuel has led many to compromise morals in the workplace, take performance-enhancing drugs in sports, lie on resumes, and cheat on exams, as well as countless other ethical and moral indiscretions. Are you fueled by the desire for money so you can buy that new house, vehicle, or boat? Are you fueled by the desire to ensure your child gets that sports scholarship or wins the weekend tournament? Is it the desire to retire comfortably that fuels you day in and day out, or is it the desire just to be wanted by another and have attention from this world?

In the following pages, let's take some time and look at the premium fuel that should drive the believer's life. Multiple motivations are often at work in any of our daily activities. This chapter doesn't dismiss that reality, but it does offer a look into God's ultimate design. God provides us with an underlying motivation that should drive all other motives in living out the holy life to which he has called all his children. Now, if you are still reading this book and you are not a follower of Christ, I encourage you to think about what fuels your life as well; however, to get this fuel, you have to give your life to Jesus. Surrendering your life to Jesus is a big decision, one that I pray you will consider and choose today.

The Good Stuff

The prophet Isaiah told us a lot about having the right motivation for our lives. Isaiah 42:1–4 reveals a God-given prophecy concerning the coming Messiah who would deliver all God's people. This prophecy was fulfilled in Matthew 12:15-21. Isaiah 42:5–9 then reminds us that God is the creator who gives life to all humanity. As Creator, God has commissioned his covenant people to evangelize the nations. From here, the author progresses in Isaiah 42:10–13 to declare that God's creation has a responsibility to sing and glorify his name because of the very nature of who God is. He is a glorious God. Then, in Isaiah 42:14–17, the tone of the text seems to change dramatically. A judgment is delivered because God's creation has failed to acknowledge him as supreme above all others and to worship him exclusively. God's people are specifically mentioned in judgment because they particularly knew better than to neglect the LORD and worship false gods (42:18–25). The covenant people of God had seen his mighty works from their deliverance from Egypt to the many successful conquests in the Promised Land. Compared to all other nations, they are especially culpable for their idolatry. Even though we know that this text is specifically speaking to Israel as a chosen and special people of God, in light of the clear prophetic tone, God's future redemptive plans, and the references to God's global family, we can see that this text also applies to us as Christians today.

Considering the context, let's walk through the first seven verses of Isaiah 43 and see what God says our premium fuel is. Verse one reads, "But now…" Okay, time out. By opening with the word "but," Isaiah shows a contrast to what he had just written. He is declaring that, despite the fact we have been under judgment for serving false gods, despite the fact that we have been living for these lesser things, God wants us to know that he's going to do something special with us. God is going to give us a purpose and motivation for life. God is going to show us something greater.

"But now thus says the LORD, he who created you, O Jacob, he who formed you, O Israel: 'Fear not, for I have redeemed you; I have called you by name, you are mine'" (Is. 43:1). Just as God created this world, God created you and me to be his special people. He has not forgotten us in our judgment, so we do not have to be afraid. Despite the painful circumstances of our judgment, God calls us not to live in fear because he himself has provided redemption from sin. He has paid the price for our sins. He has extended forgiveness. He has maintained his commitment to us and is with us. Therefore, we can have peace even in the midst of difficult circumstances because God is committed to us and present with us.

Believe it or not, on an imperfect level, we naturally get this idea of the power of presence. We get the idea of someone's presence helping calm us, even if we don't understand the purpose behind our painful experiences. Have you ever been with a parent and young child right before the child is to have a serious surgery? The parent will almost always be sitting on the edge of the bed or in a chair right beside the child. When the nurse comes in and starts preparing IV needles, medicine, and bags, the parent will often hold the child's hand and say, "Look at me. It's going to be okay. I'm right here." Now, could the surgery be stopped? Yes, but the parent knows that something greater is at stake. So it is in our text in Isaiah 43. God is reminding us in the midst of our hardship that we are his, he is with us, he has redeemed us, and he has a purpose for us. All we need to do is trust him! One author commenting on this verse wrote, "Much can be endured if we have a sense of destiny borne out of particular identity. Strip that away from us, and we think going on in life is hardly worth it."[22]

Isaiah continues, "When you pass through the waters, I will be with you; and through the rivers, they shall not overwhelm you; when you walk through fire you shall not be burned, and the flame shall not consume you" (43:2). Notice this prophetic text began by emphatically stating *"When* you pass through the waters", not *"If* you pass through the waters…"*. In other words, the question is never "if" difficulty will come, but simply "when" it will come. God

---

[22]John N. Oswalt, *The Book of Isaiah: Chapters 40-66*, NICOT (Grand Rapids: Eerdmans, 1998), 137.

is revealing to us that he will be present to guide and comfort us in the midst of painful circumstances.[23] God's purposes will surpass the trails we face, and nothing the enemy throws at us will destroy us as God's people. God's people will prevail through all kinds of trials. Hasn't history shown us that God's people have persevered through horrendous attacks, and they are still here? Certainly. But notice in this text, God tells us something that should be of great comfort to every believer:

- Trials will come.

- These trials are purposeful.

- God is with us in the trial.

If you still haven't trusted in Jesus as your Savior, please realize that you will still go through trials. The difference is that you will endure them on your own without the redemptive purposes and presence of God. Not believing in God doesn't spare you from trials; it simply robs you of hope. In fact, believe it or not, God may be using trials in your life precisely because he is trying to get your attention and draw you to receive the salvation he lovingly longs for you to receive. Trails can be acts of God's love. Look at it this way—if you won the Publishers Clearing House Sweepstakes, would you fall on your knees and start following Jesus, or would you go on a spending spree? Conversely, if your doctor told you that the CAT scan found a mass and you need to have further testing done, what are you most likely to do, start praying and asking for prayer, or go on a spending spree? If you are like most people, you will start looking for help from God, and this is precisely what God is saying through his prophet Isaiah.

Verses three and four continue together to proclaim deliverance. Look first at the personal qualities of God in verse three as "your God" and "your Savior." "For I am the LORD your God, the Holy One of Israel, your Savior. I give Egypt as your ransom, Cush and

---

[23]This idea is emphasized in other passages such as Psalm 23:4.

Seba in exchange for you" (Is. 43:3). God sacrificed for his people. In Isaiah's context, we see he gave Egypt, Cush, and Seba in exchange for his people. For us today, we know that he gave Jesus as the sacrificial lamb slain on our behalf (Is. 53:5–6; John 1:29). Obtaining his people came with a cost. We often make the mistake of thinking that redemption was free, that spiritual freedom was just given to believers. That's not the case. Make no mistake here. Just as physical redemption comes at a price, so does spiritual redemption. Spiritual redemption is freely offered but came at a great cost. God has provided redemption from sin and death. He has provided redemption from the captivity of this world so that whoever receives his gift can have a relationship with him. This deliverance came through Jesus, who was offered as a sacrifice on our behalf to redeem us from sin and death and restore us to a relationship with God. Salvation may be freely offered, but it came at a considerable price. Here's an example. Brian, a seven-year-old boy, was walking through an antique store with his parents. While his parents were looking at a dresser, he saw this very expensive, decorative vase. He just couldn't help himself. He had to touch it. As he did, the vase began to wobble on its base. Brian watched in horror as the vase fell off its base and smashed into pieces on the hard tile floor. The noise resonated throughout the store as Brian's parents and the store owner ran over to see what had happened. Brian was crying. He was terrified over what had just occurred, as well as scared about what would happen next. The owner asked if everything was okay. The price of the rare vase was clearly beyond what the parents could afford. The owner looked at the terrified boy and his parents. Then out of compassion he said, "I'll take care of this. Don't worry about it." Now, Brian and his parents may have been freed from the cost of the expensive vase, but the vase wasn't free. The owner graciously absorbed the cost. It was free to them, but their freedom still came at a high price to the owner. That's what God did for his people. He absorbed the cost of redemption. Why? "Because you are precious in my eyes, and honored, and I love you, I give men in return for you, peoples in exchange for your life" (Is. 43:4). Look at the adoring and compassionate character of God here. He says we are "precious," "honored," and "loved" by him. He says he will redeem our lives. Assuredly, God is speaking of how he has sacrificed other nations in the redemption of his people Israel; however, this message also speaks to believers today.[24] Did God not sacrifice for us? Did God not sacrifice his own Son for us? God's sacrifice on our behalf shows us how precious we are, how honored we are, and how much he loves us (John 3:16).

After describing God's redeeming work, Isaiah continues to remind us again of God's comforting presence and providential timing. God will gather all his children to himself at the right time. "Fear not, for I am with you; I will bring your offspring from the east, and from the west I will gather you. I will say to the north, Give up, and to the south, Do not withhold; bring my sons from afar and my daughters from the end of the earth" (Is. 43:5–6). This same wording is used by Jesus in Matthew 8:11 in describing the inclusion of non-Jewish people brought into this wonderful, covenant relationship with God. God's people will be composed of all the nations, which means that this text also applies to us. Just look at the command of God in Isaiah 43:5–6, which ensures his children are brought to him. If you are a parent, you can understand this concept. Most parents would move heaven and earth for to save their children. That's an interesting phrase, isn't it? "Move heaven and earth." Well, God moved a piece of heaven to earth by sending Jesus to die so that we might have a relationship with him as his child. He rescued us as his children from death and hell by paying the "wages of sin" on our behalf (Rom. 6:23).

The section concludes with a qualification. Up to this point in the text, it has all been about what God did for us, but now God reveals his purpose for us. Having been created, called, and redeemed by

---

[24]See, Oswalt, *Isaiah*, 140. It seems Isaiah is referencing God's literal defeat of these various nations through Sennacherib who then sought to come against Hezekiah; however, this prophecy is ultimately demonstrated in God giving Christ (2 Cor 5:21) who became our sin sacrifice.

God, he reveals the why. God will bring together "everyone who is called by my name, *whom I created for my glory*, whom I formed and made" (Is. 43:7). [25] Why did God create us, provide for us, sustain us, call us, and redeem us? He did it for his glory. We exist to bring glory to our redeeming God. Thus, it is our privilege to live in a way that honors and glorifies God. It is also our privilege to reflect to others the reality that God is glorious and worthy of everyone's worship and affection. Our motivation, our premium fuel that should drive every aspect of our lives, is living for the glory of God. God's glory is fuel for the journey and should be the ultimate motivation in all that we do.

Cleaning the Tank

I have a good friend who lives on Pine Mountain in Remlap, Alabama. One day, I went over to his home and saw him working on an old truck behind his garage. I walked around to hang out and asked him what he was doing. He explained that he was removing the gas tank on the truck. "Why?" I asked. He explained that the truck had some "old fuel in the tank that had gone bad and had to be removed." As a result, he had to clean out the system and then put fresh fuel in that tank so that it would run properly.

Here's the reality. Some of us have been putting bad fuel in our tanks for years. We have been motivated by lesser gods and living for lesser glories. We are motivated by pleasure and comfort so that we can retire at a certain age. We are driven to make the sports team in order to please our parents or prove to the world that we are successful. The love of money motivates much of our weekly physical and mental activities as we strive for more possessions and then enjoy the many comforts and pleasures they bring. We are driven by the desire to have the approval of others allowing what other people think to impact many areas of our lives. We allow fear to fuel us daily. We fear our financial future. We fear losing our jobs.

---

[25]Emphasis added.

We fear disappointing our spouse or messing up our children. We fear the safety of loved ones as they travel, and these fears drive us.

Just pause to think about what is motivating your life? What fuel drives you? One of the greatest problems with bad fuel in our lives is that initially we don't really know the difference. We think that so long as life is running okay, using bad fuel is "good enough." It may get us through today, but why settle for just existing, just chugging along on "good enough", when you know there is something out there that promises a better today and a better tomorrow? Why just keep using bad fuel? Many of us have a tank full of bad fuel, and as a result, we need to clean out the tank, which takes hard work, discipline, and time. So, what follows are three related self-examination questions that will help us on the road to cleaning out our tanks and preparing our minds and hearts to live driven by a desire to see the glory of God manifested in and through us.

1. Will I accept that God loves me and created me to be his?

For the person still reading who is not a Christian, it all starts here. A life-altering relationship with God starts by trusting in Jesus as the one who redeems you from your sin and rescues you to be a child of God. However, the truth that God loves me and created me to be his doesn't cease being relevant when I become a Christian. This truth is relevant every day of our lives, and we would do well to remember it. Think of how often we are distracted by the ways of the world and driven off course because we are seeking love and significance, a love and significance that have already been given to us by God. We have a purpose, and it starts by identifying the all-satisfying love of God and the reality that we were redeemed to be his. Admittedly, many of us believe God loves us and created us to be his. We just need to grow in that belief. The reality of God's special love in our lives has transformed many parts of our motivational tanks, but there is still work to be done, depths of belief to be discovered, and further surrender to be made.

2. Will I accept that God has given me a purpose in life and that that purpose is to live for his glory, which means I seek to honor him and represent him rightly to others?

God didn't save us to just mark time in life until he comes back or we die and go to be with him. No, he rescued us from the dominion of darkness to be salt and light in this world (Matt. 5:13–16; Col. 1:13–14). We have purpose here and now. As we live out that purpose, we are literally pushing back the darkness of this world and bringing the dominion of the kingdom of God to bear.

Unfortunately, all too often, we allow the pain of this world to distract us from the purposes of God. As a result, we begin to live for relief from pain versus living to proclaim the glory of a gracious, good, and great God. Can you relate to this tendency we all have? How are you trying to relieve your pain? Where are you trying to find purpose and significance in this world, through your calling from God or the fallen circumstances of this world? For example, you don't have to cut your body to try and dull the pain because your circumstances don't define you. You are loved by a gracious heavenly Father who has paid a tremendous price to redeem you. Your failed marriage or business doesn't define you, but your relationship to God in Jesus does. Your infertility doesn't define you. That molestation you experienced doesn't define who you are as a beloved child of the King. Whatever your pain, whatever your story, God has a purpose for your life. Even if you are just bored with your normal, usual, everyday experience, you don't have to live as if your lot in life is to be insignificant to the world. Do your mundane activity to the glory of God as you exercise dominion over your part of creation (Gen. 1:28; Ps. 115:16; Col. 3:16). He has redeemed you from the pit (Ps. 40:2). God has established you in Jesus, given you a purpose, and enabled you to live a life of glory representing him to the world. You have a new name as a child of God, a new nature, and a new purpose.

As we grow in our understanding of the purposes of God and our identity as a child of God, we are better equipped to live in a way that brings glory to God and points others to him. When we accept that our actions matter in bringing glory to God, not just on Sunday mornings in church but in every way in every place at every moment of every day, it changes the way we live our lives. The way you and I live matters! When our neighbor builds his fence on our property line, the way we act matters. When someone cuts us off in traffic or takes forever in the grocery checkout line in front of us, the way we act matters. The way we speak to our parents, spouse, or kids matters. The way we conduct business or balance spreadsheets matters. What we do to close a sale matters.

3. Will I work to let the glory of God be the fuel that drives my life?

It is work to discipline our minds in this way. It takes time. However, the more we train our minds to focus on our purpose to live for the glory of God, and the more we allow our identity to be defined by our relationship with God and not with the world, the more natural it will be for us to make God-honoring decisions and represent him rightly. We must discipline our lives to be motivated, not out of a desire to preserve or promote self but because our hope is in God. As Paul explained to his young protégé, Timothy:

> "Have nothing to do with godless myths and old wives' tales; rather, **train yourself to be godly**. For physical training is of some value, but godliness has value for all things, holding promise for both the present life and the life to come. This is a trustworthy saying that deserves full acceptance. That is why we labor and strive, because we have put our hope in the living God, who is the Savior of all people, and especially of those who believe."

1 Tim. 4:7–10[26]

Our all-consuming purpose should be to live for the glory of God as a result of the hope we have through the life, death, and resurrection of our savior Jesus. This God-given purpose is to motivate us in the most private and mundane aspects of our lives.

---

[26]Emphasis added.

As we mow the grass, we exercise dominion for the glory of God. As we make love to our spouse, we do it for the glory of God. As we clean up our workstations, we do it for the glory of God. As we show kindness to a coworker or teacher, we do it for the glory of God. As we study for an exam so that we can do our best with the talents he has given us, we do it for the glory of God. As we talk to a friend in crisis about the saving work and hope found only in Jesus, we do it for the glory of God. You get the idea. As Paul concisely statess, "So whether you eat or drink or whatever you do, do it all for the glory of God" (1 Cor. 10:31).

Final Consideration

What difference would it make if we collectively accepted this truth? Just think how people would respond if they noticed such a change in our lives that they asked what's going on, and we told them, "You might think I'm crazy, but God has so changed my heart and life that I am living for him to glorify his name." How might people perceive the church if we collectively abandoned a mediocre Christianity that was all about us and authentically lived a Christian life that was motivated by the glory of God? That is the call of every believer in Christ. If you are not a believer in Christ, join in. It's a great ride, and I'm sorry for those times when our hypocrisy has kept you from seeing God's glory. But then again, the real issue is how amazing God is, not how amazing are those he created to reflect his glory. He really is an amazing God. Don't let our failures keep you from him. That's why we needed grace in the first place. He's a glorious God who has graciously saved us.

Questions for Reflection:

Can you describe a time in which your desire to impress others led you to make a bad decision? What was the outcome?

Think of something you did recently that brought fear, shame, or regret. What motivated your decision to act, speak, or think in such a way?

How does understanding God's love for you help you live for his glory? What are some practical ways you can remind yourself this coming week of God's love for you?

How would this past week look different if you were consistently living for the glory of God? What are some things you can do for this upcoming week to help you live more consistently for God's glory?

CHAPTER 5
IDENTITY: DEFINED BY GOD

Who am I?

If there's one consistent theme in the Bourne movies, it's Jason Bourne's quest to uncover his true identity. In the first movie, Bourne stops at a diner and confesses his bewilderment to his new acquaintance Marie. He can't understand why he's watching the exits and the people in the restaurant, why he can tell the license plate numbers of all the cars outside, how he knows he could run for half a mile at this altitude before his hands would start to shake. And then Bourne asks a crucial question. "How can I know that and not know who I am?"

As viewers, we don't say, "Who cares who you are?" We don't act like his identity crisis is irrelevant. Everyone thinks Bourne *should* discover who he is. We realize that our identities matter. The reason Bourne acts in such odd (and impressively violent) ways is rooted in his identity, in who he *really* is. And the truth is, we're no different.

Before moving forward, we should stop and define the word identity. It's an abstract concept that psychologists only labeled in the last century. For our purposes, the psychological definitions aren't the focus. We're using the word "identity" to describe your characteristics, personal history, attributes, personality, and habits all rolled together into one. Your identity is like a taco with distinct ingredients that combine to create your unique flavor. And identities are important because the way we define ourselves will determine how we live. In short, *whatever defines you directs you.*

67

You won't see the term 'identity' in most English Bible translations, but the principle remains true in Scripture: whatever defines you directs you. That's why God often changes people's names. God changes Abram's name to Abraham in Genesis 17 when he formalizes the covenant with the sign of circumcision. Jacob becomes Israel and Simon becomes Peter at critical junctures in their spiritual lives. Jesus even labels his disciples 'little faith.' The point is, the way we define ourselves—especially a person's name in the ancient world—impacts the things we do and the trajectory of our lives. Your identity determines the path you take in life, your view of right and wrong, your purpose for existence. Whatever defines you directs you!

So, as we move forward, we must do the hard work of self-examination. Few people enjoy deep introspection, but it is vital. I'm (Matt) not an emotional man (at least not outwardly), nor do I like to sit and talk about my feelings. I'm not a hippie. But I know how critical it is to examine the way I view myself. So, you and I must begin by realizing how we presently define ourselves in order to discern the need to understand our God-given identities. Let's start with some labels—both good and bad—that often define us, and then we will consider how these definitions direct our actions.

Label-makers

One destructive but prevalent label is "failure." Few people ever say out loud, "I'm a failure," but many broadcast this self-identity in other ways. Some refuse to try new things because they might not succeed. I can't take that new job because what if I don't fit in and they fire me? Thanks for asking me to teach that Bible study, but I'm really not educated enough. I'd love to learn to swim, but I've never been good in water. People who make statements like these see themselves as failures, as people who don't want to risk confirming what they know to be true. Sadly, when we identify ourselves as failures, it causes us to refuse to try anything new—to refuse to grow! This label demands that we avoid risks, seeing them not as opportunities to mature but as short cuts to more failure. They are stuck. Only an identity change can restore their mobility.

Unlike failure, not all labels are bad, though even positive labels can become distorted when taken to the extreme. Take someone whose identity is inseparably tied to a career. Wanting success in your career is not sinful, but obsession with it is. When your career becomes your idol (something you care more about than God), you don't care who you stomp on to climb to the top. People become means to your desired end. Even your own family can get left behind as you work eighteen-hour days to make sure you're promoted. And when you're home, you aren't present. You're on your laptop while your spouse tries to engage in conversation. The kids know not to interact with you unless they want to bear your anger and frustration. If that isn't bad enough, when you suffer job loss or miss a promotion, your world falls apart. You said to yourself, "If I don't become a CEO, I won't know who I am." And now you're lost. By the way, even pastors struggle with this. Some see themselves foremost as pastors and define their value by their congregations' attendance trends, giving patterns, and words of affirmation. Yet even the identity of 'pastor' is insufficient on its own.

Maybe at this point, you're thinking of people you know who struggle with these labels, but we haven't hit home yet. So, what about using our relationships as an identity marker? Do you see yourself as a mom, dad, or spouse above all other labels? Before I was a dad, I thought it was weird that parents were so into their kids. I thought, "I really didn't care about your kid's 'art,' so lay off the Instagram posts." But when my perfect angel of a daughter Rylie was born, it all clicked. I realized I could easily make this child my obsession. But there's a problem. Now that she is three years old, it's clear that Rylie is a little sinner—a delightful child but imperfect nonetheless. And it is unfair to make her, or any other imperfect human being, my identity. It's too much pressure on a person to live up to my impossibly high expectations. So, when my identity is dependent upon her perfection (or how much she likes me or, one day, how much time my adult daughter spends with me), it will inevitably destroy both of our identities. We will both feel like failures.

Maybe you find your identity in your appearance. Now, I know all of the guys just checked out. But the truth is, men are just as entangled in our appearance, though maybe in a different way. We may not spend as much time in front of the mirror, but many of us do define ourselves by our appearance. I know guys who have had the same haircut since the Reagan era. If that's you, would you "feel like yourself" if, heaven forbid, your barber gave you swoopy bangs? And what about men in my neck of the woods who wouldn't be caught dead without their perfectly starched wranglers and snakeskin cowboy boots that cost more than my whole wardrobe? My point is that men and women are both at risk on this one.

Now, I am not a woman, have never been a woman, and would never be so foolish to claim that I understand the vastly superior mind of a woman. But I do know that the greatest struggle for some comes in the checkout line at the grocery store as you wait for the couponer up ahead to wrap it up. In that moment, you're surrounded by glossy magazine covers picturing the world's most perfect women—or so you think. Deep down, I think everyone realizes that Photoshop can make a monster into a super model in the time it takes to microwave popcorn. And yet so many compare themselves to these (overly) perfect images. Do you? Do you ever feel like you're not good enough—maybe not even good enough for your own spouse—because you don't look like a magazine cover? Or what about this. Do you ever belittle others to make yourself feel better? It feels good to find and proclaim the flaws in people we feel inferior to. But all our nitpicking does is demonstrate that our identity is tied to appearance.

There is one more label worth considering. Do you define yourself by your past? As you've read this book, our hope is that you've placed your faith in Jesus as your Savior and Lord. Scripture tells us that when we trust in Christ, we become a new creation. Yet, for many of us, the skeletons hiding in the closet of the 'old creation' are hard to leave behind. Maybe you believe in Jesus, but you can't get beyond the mistakes, even the evils, of your past. Do you live in fear that someone will discover what you did back then? Would people be horrified if your past was exposed? You still identify yourself as an "abuser" rather than as a "new creation." Maybe the label "addict" hangs over you, and every time someone talks to you at church, you assume they only see you as a user. For others, your spouse left, despite your protests, and you feel like all you'll ever be is a divorcee. And while you appreciate the forgiveness offered by Jesus, you refuse to serve your church family or accept a leadership position. You're too worried about what people think of your past. In your eyes, you *are* your past and nothing more.

These labels just scratch the surface, but they illustrate a principle. *Whatever defines us directs us.* The way we label ourselves will determine how we live, think, and interact with others. So, before moving on to the way God defines his children, I challenge you to pause. Yes, I know you only have so much time to read this book, and there are other things to do. But I beg you to stop and answer this question honestly. *Other than God, what defines me?* Where do you find your identity? Do you identify with one, two, or all of the labels already mentioned? Ponder these questions. Then, when you're ready, move on to the good news, to the high esteem God has for his children.

The Born (Again) Identity

The letter known as 1 Peter was written to Christians suffering with an identity crisis. Peter writes to an audience suffering persecution, but not the kind you might expect. Other than pockets of violent persecution that usually centered in Rome, the first century church more often encountered social ostracism, financial oppression, and societal scorn. In other words, the friends and family members of new Christians would reject them, costing them relational and business networks. And it should be no surprise that Christians living in these conditions would start to question themselves. "I thought I was doing what was right, but now I'm suffering. Does this mean God isn't for me? Am I actually outside of God's favor?"

This is the age-old question of why bad things happen to good people—even God's people? At the root, though, is a question of identity. Does God really care about me? Do I wear the label "loved by God"?

Responding to these questions, 1 Peter 2:9–10 lists six defining characteristics for his audience of believers. These descriptions define the church as a whole but should also define individual believers in all times and places. Like a good pastor, Peter refers back to Scripture (the Old Testament) and its descriptions of Israel in order to highlight God's high view of his people. And since these ancient labels define us, we will also consider how they direct us. We will see that the right labels enable us to live rightly.

Let's read together. "But you are a chosen race, a royal priesthood, a holy nation, a people for his own possession, that you may proclaim the excellencies of him who called you out of darkness into his marvelous light. Once you were not a people, but now you are God's people; once you had not received mercy, but now you have received mercy" (1 Pet. 2:9–10 ESV).

Peter first labels believers as a 'chosen race.' This may seem like an odd description, especially since the church is composed of people from many nations and races. But remember that Peter is utilizing Old Testament imagery here in order to highlight the identity of believers. So, let's focus on the word "chosen." In the realm of theology, the language of election or "being chosen" carries a number of important connotations that are beyond the scope of this book (being more like "square six" than "square one"). In other words, the term 'chosen' can be controversial and complex, but I think Peter's point here is simple. You are not God's B-team. Peter does not want his suffering audience to believe they are God's second string, the people God tolerates but doesn't really love. And like the original audience, we often assume there is a class of believers who are God's A-team: pastors, full-time missionaries, Bible scholars, and so on. We think these are the people God really loves and uses, and we're just scenery. Or worse, we sometimes act like we had to beg God to accept us or force him to save us. The implication is that God didn't really want to save someone like me. He just felt obligated.

But Peter dispels both of these false assumptions. We don't have to wait until we think we've arrived or we're more deserving of being on God's A-team. No, you have a new identity already. You are chosen. The very God who created and sustains all things has chosen the Church as his people and has chosen you, believer. I know you are not a second-class Christian because there is no such thing. And this new definition should direct you to get off the sidelines. No longer do you need to wait to pursue God until x, y, or z occurs. You don't need to clean yourself up before you *really* follow Christ. You are chosen. You don't have to memorize the entire Bible in the original languages before you teach Scripture to children because you are chosen. You don't have to step back so the 'professionals' can do it because you, too, are chosen. Peter could have stopped with this life-changing label, but he goes on.

Second, believers in Jesus Christ are a royal priesthood. We don't really have royalty in America, nor do we encounter many priests (at least priests in the Old Testament sense). Because we are not acquainted with these roles, this might be a label we're tempted to skip over. But, these roles are critical in the Old Testament for several reasons. Priests and kings were mediators between God and his people. The priests would take the Israelites' sacrifices and offer them to God, bridging the gap between God and his people. In a similar way, the Old Testament kings were the ones who received God's instructions for the nation and carried them out. In a sense, then, they mediated the leadership of God for Israel. Because of their mediating roles, these figures gained high status within the community. Moses and Aaron, for example, were from the priestly tribe (the Levites), and kings like David and Solomon clearly were men of influence. So, when Peter uses the phrase 'royal priesthood,' he implies not only that believers are meant to connect people to God but also that Christians are high-status people in God's eyes. Our society may view us as poor and powerless, but we are God's top tier—the upper echelon.

Maybe you're asking how identifying ourselves as high-status people directs how we live now. Well, thanks for asking! The truth is that high-status people don't care what the little people think of them. Take Lebron James, who most think is the greatest basketball player since Michael Jordan. Lebron has lead teams to the NBA finals multiple times, makes more money than I could imagine, and has dined with presidents. I am pastor who is not the best basketball player in my church, not even in my own family (my wife is a baller). So, if I decide to criticize Lebron's jump shot, he doesn't care. It makes no difference if I love him or hate him because he's important, and I'm a nobody. My opinion is irrelevant. In the same way, while we care about the lost world, their opinions of us are irrelevant. We are high-status people in God's eyes, so we don't obsess over whether our unsaved friends and neighbors respect our beliefs. If they mock us, who cares? If they ostracize us, we remain connected to God. The result is that we can ignore how the world label's us, rejecting their definitions as insignificant. We are a royal priesthood to God.

Peter's third label is one that guilt-ridden Christians have a hard time accepting. We are a holy nation. This might be a good time to re-read the earlier chapter on holiness, because the concept is difficult. I have known believers who refused to sing songs proclaiming their holiness in Christ because they don't feel holy. But Peter calls the church a holy nation. When God looks at the believer in Jesus, he sees Christ and declares the believer to be holy. Whether you feel holy or not, you are holy in Jesus Christ.

But with this label comes a high expectation. In fact, 1 Peter 1:14–16 articulates the expectation that God's people will imitate his holiness. God's demand is simple but not easy. "Since I have made you holy," God says, "act like it." This is one of the closest correlations we've seen between how God defines us and how the definition directs us. A holy nation should strive to be holy, not by always asking how far is too far but by asking, "How close to God's holiness can I come?" We are so busy looking for the shoreline that we don't enjoy the lake as God commands. Quit looking for boundaries, and enjoy the safe zone—the middle. Instead of moving as close to sin as God will allow, we should strive toward God's holiness, trusting his Spirit to enable us.

Fourth, we are God's possession. The individualists among us don't want to be anyone's possession, but they forget the goodness of the one who possess us. So, I like to think of the Church as God's trophy wife. We didn't do anything to earn God's favor or to deserve our position, but God has set us upon on a pedestal. I imagine God crying out, "Look, world, at my beautiful bride, who I will love and cherish forever. Just look at her!" The unfortunate irony, however, is that we're not always so proud of our generous God.

For me, salesmen are my downfall. They have been trained to ask, "So, what do you do?" My immediate response, if I'm being honest, is usually to duck the question. I don't want to admit I'm a pastor, partly because I don't want to have to be nice. I also think salesmen are like sharks sensing blood when they hear the word 'pastor'—as if the grace of God demands that I buy their product at the highest price. But, honestly, there's also a part of me that simply isn't as proud of my God as I should be. So, I sometimes worm my way out of the conversation or change the subject rather than admit that I belong to a holy, generous, patient God. The label Peter gives to his audience is vital, then, because it directs us to proudly display God. If I am truly the possession of God, I should boast in Him. Peter mentions the proper response to these labels next, but we'll come back to it after we finish defining the believer's identity.

The fifth label appears anticlimactic at this point in the list, but it illustrates an important truth undergirding the labels. We are God's people, and God intends for us to function as a group. We will talk more about the church in a later chapter, but here it is worth acknowledging that there is no such thing as a lone-ranger Christian. I often hear people claim that they like Jesus but want nothing to do with the church. But we collectively are God's people—the Church. God did not design for you to follow him alone. We are vital to one another, just as each bodily organ requires all other organs to survive. Brains are important but useless without hearts and lungs. Feet are great, but a lone foot isn't terribly effective. The reality of the corporate body has been lurking in the background of terms such 'race' and 'nation' but is highlighted in this simple label: God's people.

So how does the label impact the way we live? I think it demands that we pursue unity. Being part of a church is hard because of all of the people. I am an introvert by nature, so I find it even more difficult than some to connect within the church. But I also believe that my church family is essential and that they are worth the effort. If we are a part of God's people, it demands that we pursue unity. We must love each other when it's hard. Believers should display the fruit of the Spirit toward one another. We should forgive and reconcile. Living up to this label demands that we strive to build up the church and show the world that we are God's people.

The final label Peter mentions encapsulates the Gospel message that we are recipients of mercy. At one time, we were not under the mercy of God, but now we are. We once lived without knowing the kindness of God, without living out his purpose for us, without enjoying His favor. But, because of the death and resurrection of Jesus, everything changed. Today, if you have confessed faith in Jesus as your Savior and Lord, you are a recipient of mercy. God's mercy motivates all that we do as believers. We worship in response to the mercy of God, proclaiming his greatness with our entire lives. We are generous people because of the generous mercy of God. When we suffer, we don't lose hope because God's mercy matters more.

Peter emphasizes one more implication of God's mercy in 1 Peter 5:5–6. Recipients of mercy should be humble. If God's mercy—His undeserved kindness—is the reason for our status, then we should be a humble people. We should stop acting like we're super Christians, walking around our churches with puffed chests and upturned noses. Churches should not take credit for the growth God brings (see 1 Corinthians 3). In a different vein, we as Christians should stop expending so much energy trying to look like we are doing well. Our pride prevents us from admitting that we struggle, that we're lonely, that we haven't defeated our sin natures. But humble people don't need to look perfect because it is enough to be recipients of mercy. If our identity is rooted in God's mercy, there is no room for pride, self-sufficiency, or selfishness. A recipient of mercy should live humbly, because whatever defines us directs us.

Training for the Fight

The six labels Peter names in 1 Peter 2:9–10 change everything. We are not God's B-team but are chosen by Him. The Church lives as high-status people because we are a royal priesthood. We are a holy nation who should strive to imitate God's holiness, and, as God's trophy wife, we must display him proudly. These labels are corporate because we are God's people, the Church. And, since we have received mercy, humility should follow. But simply believing these labels is not enough.

You see, every day when you drive to work, open a magazine at the doctor's office, or pull up Hulu, the world is trying to define you. Advertisers are telling you who you are and what you need. Billboards are trying to tell you how to live and think. Movies tell you to be individualistic and self-sufficient. We as believers, then, must make a focused effort to allow God to label us. So, *will you fight to let God define you so He can direct you*? Passivity is not enough. If we ignore this issue or read this chapter and assume our identity is now corrected, we will be defined by the world. We have to fight daily to label ourselves according to God's word, battling against the untrue definitions that surround us.

The reason your identity is essential is because you aren't the only one affected. We skipped over Peter's purpose statement wedged in the middle of the list: "that you may proclaim the excellencies of him who called you out of darkness into his marvelous light." We have a God-given purpose to proclaim Him, to tell others that He has brought us out of darkness. By proclaiming God, we give Him the glory He so clearly deserves. But, proclamation also benefits those who haven't yet seen the marvelous light, telling them that something better is out there. Unbelievers are watching us, and they often perceive how we identify ourselves better than we do. So, to glorify God by enlightening others requires us to accept our new identities. The guilty, prideful, or embarrassed Christian will not proclaim how excellent God is. Only when we have a right definition of who we are in Christ will we proclaim God's greatness with our lives and words.

As you begin fighting to allow God-given labels to shape your new identity in Him, let me offer some practical advice. Begin making a list this week of ways God labels you. Write down labels and associated Bible passages so that you can regularly pray through them. This chapter is not going to change you. Only God can, and His most common instrument is a regular diet of His word. I like to keep lists like these on my phone so that, no matter where I am, if I sense another voice overtaking God's, I can pull out my phone and fight. When your past starts to overwhelm you, read 2 Corinthians 5 and be reminded that God labels you as a new creation. Your past no longer defines you. When you start to doubt whether God really loves you, remember that 1 Peter 2:9–10 says that you are a recipient of mercy. Your identity in God matters, so fight for it!

Questions for Reflection

If you were to pick two or three labels that have defined you in the past, what would they be? Why have these defined you?

What influences your sense of identity? Are there worldly elements that impact how you think about yourself?

Which of the labels from 1 Peter 2 impacts you the most? What is so meaningful about that particular label?

How would it change the way you act if you defined yourself the way Peter defines you?

What does it mean to "proclaim the excellencies" of God? How do our God-given labels enable us to proclaim him more effectively?

CHAPTER 6
POWER: ENABLED BY GOD

Excuses

It was 1997. I (Adam) had just been honorably discharged from the United States Marine Corps. My hair still resembled military personnel as I walked into the doors of Southeastern Bible College in Birmingham, Alabama, and applied for school. I never thought of myself as an academic person, but I knew God had a call on my life. I also knew that I needed some help, so at the advice of a local pastor, I walked in and enrolled. A few weeks later, I was sitting in my first Bible course. The first day of class the professor had us open our Bibles to Jeremiah 17:9—"The heart is deceitful above all things and beyond cure. Who can understand it?" Then he had everyone repeat a phrase that would be the mantra throughout the entire course: "I'm a dirty, rotten, stinking, sinner." Now, as an aside, I fully understand what the professor was attempting to accomplish. Notwithstanding the intention, what I came away with was a) you are saved by grace, but b) you are still a sinner, so c) you will constantly fail! Since I was a "dirty, rotten, stinking sinner," I began to believe I was a failure who would inevitably give in to certain sins. So instead of confessing and dealing with sin biblically, I worked harder at hiding my sins. My focus was on keeping people from discovering what a moral failure I was. After all, I'm stuck. This is who I am. I'm broken and messed up. At this point in my life, I was publically preparing for pastoral ministry, but privately, I struggled greatly with anger and pornography. They were literally ruining my life because I felt trapped and powerless. I felt saved for a future glory but worthless in the here and now.

Do you ever feel that way? I believe some of you do. Over the years of ministry, I have had the privilege of ministering to thousands of people. My wife and I have heard their stories. We've listened, laughed, and cried with them. In doing so, we regularly hear statements like:

- ❖ I want to be a godly spouse, but…

- ❖ I want to be a good worker, but…

- ❖ I want to stop being lazy, but…

- ❖ I want to stop being so selfish, but…

These people then go on to explain why they can't live the life to which God has called them. They go on to explain how they are helpless and powerless. Can you relate? Do you ever feel that you are stuck in a behavioral rut? Do you ever wonder how you could ever live up to God's expectations? Do you sometimes feel helpless?

Just to be clear, as incredible as my first Bible professor was, he was wrong. Studying God's word over the years, I found that in Christ we are no longer dirty, rotten, stinking, sinners, but blood-bought saints of the Most-High God who are empowered and equipped for victory in this world in anticipation of the world to come. Now when I hear people giving testimony of their lot in life and how they want to live for Jesus but can't, I immediately think of Ottis on the Andy Griffith show. Do you remember him? He was the town drunk. He would live sober for a while and then inevitably fall back into the bottle. He knew he shouldn't drink, but he just couldn't help himself. Then, after he had gotten drunk, Ottis walk into the Sheriff's office and lock himself up. After a night of sobering up, he'd leave, committing to try a little harder next time. This experience seems to describe so many Christians today who feel sin is inevitable. They know they shouldn't give up and give in, but they do. And, after they do, they lock themselves up in guilt and shame for a couple of days until they believe they have produced enough sorrow and paid enough penance. Eventually, they let themselves out of emotional purgatory. They walk away from the guilt and shame with a genuine commitment to try harder in their own strength. Yet, inevitably, they end up repeating the cycle.

God has an amazing resource for us to have the power to live his way. We are not defined by the heart we had before we came to Jesus. God has given us a new heart, a new identity, and a new power to walk in victory (Ezek. 36:26; 2 Cor. 5:17; Rom. 8:11). So, let's look together in the book of Galatians at this life-changing power God has given to us through the Lord Jesus.

Walking by The Spirit

The apostle Paul wrote to the church in Galatia, correcting some false views that were going around. His purpose for them, as well as for us, was to change their understanding of salvation and reorient their thinking regarding what it means to live and walk with Jesus. Paul wanted them to understand the Christian life more clearly. Galatians 5:16 then came at a pivotal point in the letter, where Paul talks about how to live the Christian life and what that looks like. If we back up to the beginning of Galatians chapter 5, we can see this more clearly. Paul writes there, "It is for freedom that Christ has set us free. Stand firm, then, and do not let yourselves be burdened again by a yoke of slavery" (5:1). Within the church in Galatia, a strong contingency of false teachers was leading people astray by saying that, in order to be a follower of Christ, you must be circumcised. These false teachers were teaching that it is through obedience to the law that the covenant relationship with God was maintained, and their teachings were creating division within the church. Paul then came along and blasted this arrogant, self-promoting approach to the spiritual life. Paul declared that Christ has set us free. Christ has fulfilled the legal demands of the law. The law in part showed us that we couldn't earn or maintain our relationship with God on our own. Jesus had to do it for us, and once we have received his provision for salvation from the condemnation brought by the law, we can rest in the freedom he brings. This freedom he secured for us delivers us from the necessity of striving to be made right with God or earn a relationship with him. Since we have been made right with God through the work of Jesus Christ, we can live for him, not through the circumcision of our flesh, but by walking in the power of the Holy Spirit. We can really love God and love our neighbor now. So Paul presented a call in the book of Galatians for us to use the freedom God brought from sin and death to love others and live out God's love.

Thus, Paul proclaims, "So" in spite of what these agitators were saying—"I say, walk by the Spirit, and you will not gratify the desires of the flesh" (Gal. 5:16). The secret to walking with power is not circumcision or any other external manifestation of salvation, but a will that submits to the Spirit of God and allows his power to work through us. In this verse, Paul is explaining how not to live for self and how to walk in powerful obedience to God.

Paul commands us to walk by the Spirit, but who is this Spirit? We see him throughout the Bible. He is present at creation (Gen. 1:1) and at Jesus' baptism (Matt. 3:16). The biblical writers showed that God sent his Spirit to, among other things,

- ❖ convict us of sin (John 16:8);

- ❖ wash away our sin at salvation and make us new (Titus 3:5);

- ❖ equip us with gifts for serving Jesus and his church (1 Cor. 12:1);

- ❖ unite us into the body of Christ (1 Cor. 12:13);

- ❖ dwell in us (John 14:16–17);

- ❖ assure us of our salvation (Rom. 8:16; 1 John 3:24);

- ❖ help us testify about the good news concerning Jesus (John 14:26; Acts 1:8);

- ❖ intercede for us before God (Rom. 8:26); and

- ❖ guide us (Rom. 8:14).

The Holy Spirit is given to us by God for our benefit. The Spirit works in us so we can live the spiritual life he has for us as his children. That being said, what did Paul mean when he wrote that we are to "walk by" this Spirit? To walk by the Spirit means to let him be our power source and the one who dictates the purpose and direction for our lives. Unless a lamp is connected to a power source, it cannot fulfill the function for which it was designed. It can serve as a paperweight, a lawn ornament, or a football pylon, but it will not light up the darkness without power. To walk by the Spirit is to follow his lead, to submit to his will, and **to do what he wants.** In other words, it's **His Way over Our Way by His Power!** And here is the point. We can! We can live God's way over our own desires if we submit to his direction and his power. We can walk by the Spirit, but we can also choose not to.

Some of us have been wallowing around in sin, moping about like we are in an episode of the Walking Dead, just trying to survive this world. Some of us have been trying to make it on our own believing that, somehow, we know best. We need to stop. The fact is that, if we would simply be honest, we would acknowledge we are failures at living godly lives on our own. We stink at it. It's time for us to quit living for ourselves and by our power. It's time for us to stop doing life our own way. It's time for us to abandon our lame excuses.

- ❖ I know I shouldn't, but…
- ❖ I know I shouldn't cheat on that exam, but…
- ❖ I know I shouldn't get that pay-per-view when I travel, but…
- ❖ I know I shouldn't dress provocatively, but…
- ❖ I know I shouldn't talk about them behind their backs, but…
- ❖ I know I shouldn't lose my temper in traffic, but
- ❖ I know I shouldn't lie on my expense report, bu

But nothing! The reality is that when we live our own way, we are communicating that we value these things over God, that we know best, and that we desire this outcome more than living connected to God and for his glory. Here's some biblical advice that's long overdue for many of us. Choose to submit to the Holy Spirit, and

- ❖ Don't cheat on the exam.

- ❖ Rip the cable out, get accountability, block the channel, ask for the TV to be removed, and don't get the pay-per-view.

- ❖ Stop trying to get attention by dressing provocatively.

- ❖ Don't slander or gossip about others.

- ❖ Wake up earlier, and you wouldn't be rushed.

- ❖ Don't cheat your employer.

All this can be done by his power when choosing his ways. You, as a Spirit-filled believer, don't have to live enslaved to sin anymore. Like Ottis in the Andy Griffith show, who finally reaches up, grabs the key just outside the cell, and lets himself out, our key is on the wall. We can stop locking ourselves in our spiritual prison. We can get out and get on with a godly life by the power of the Holy Spirit.

Paul goes on in his letter to the Galatians to share a test to help us determine whether we are submitting to the Holy Spirit's direction and power in and through our lives. Look at the last half of his sentence. "So I say, walk by the Spirit, **and you will not gratify the desires of the flesh**" (Gal. 5:16). When we submit to the power of the Spirit and follow his lead, we submit to his will, and we do what he wants over what we want. Saying "yes" to the Holy Spirit means we are at the same time saying "no" to our sinful desires—it's just that simple.

Fleshly Desires

Catch what's going on here. Paul didn't say that we will not have fleshly, ungodly desires. No! Paul says that, despite the presence of ungodly desires, we can still choose to submit to the empowering work of God's Spirit. Believers will still struggle with temptation to sin as long as they live. So long as we live in the fallen environment of the world, we will experience the desire to rebel. We will desire at times to act inappropriately, but temptation alone isn't sin. The presence of a desire to sin isn't the same as acting upon those desires and sinning. The key is what we do with temptation. Our response to temptation determines whether we are walking by the Spirit or sinning. Let's use this example. Let's say you are in the gym working out, and someone you find attractive walks by. Unintentionally, you notice. You don't stare or begin lusting, but your mind still registers that someone hot is walking by. Okay, what comes next? A desire arises. Maybe that desire is to capture that image for later "meditation," maybe it is to stare and "check the person out," or maybe it is to go and find a machine near where the person is so that you can strike up a conversation to see where things go. You know these desires are sinful, and you sense the gentle whisper of the Spirit saying, "Flee that desire. Block that image. Focus on me." The Spirit may even encourage you to leave the gym and choose purity. The question is, "Will I lust or run after God? Will I yield my desire to the Spirit and live his way over my way by his power?"

The point is pretty simple, but in case Paul wasn't clear enough, he expands the idea by giving a sample list of what it looks like to live our own way and then contrasts such living with what it looks like to live God's way. Paul starts first by showing what it looks like to live in submission to our fleshly desires.

> "For the flesh desires what is contrary to the Spirit, and the Spirit what is contrary to the flesh. They are in conflict with each other, so that you are not to do whatever you want. But if you are led by the Spirit, you are not under the law. The acts of the flesh are obvious: sexual immorality, impurity and debauchery; idolatry and witchcraft; hatred, discord, jealousy, fits of rage, selfish ambition, dissensions, factions and envy; drunkenness, orgies, and the like. I warn you, as I did before, that those who live like this will not inherit the kingdom of God."
>
> Galatians 5:17–21

As we read through the letter to the Galatians, Paul's point becomes clear. Actions such as those he describes in this passage flow from ungodly desires. If these ungodly desires are the unrepentant pattern of our lives, then we are not children of God. Let me say that again. Paul writes that if our life is unrepentantly characterized by such actions—in other words, if these are the things we often enjoy doing with no thought of God—then we do not have the Spirit of God. We are not believers in Jesus. "But," in contrast to giving in to these fleshly desires, we can submit to the Spirit.

> *"But the fruit of the Spirit is love, joy, peace, forbearance, kindness, goodness, faithfulness, gentleness and self-control. Against such things there is no law. Those who belong to Christ Jesus have crucified the flesh with its passions and desires. Since we live by the Spirit, let us keep in step with the Spirit."*

Galatians 5:22–25

As we submit to the leading of the Spirit, the fruit of his presence is produced in our lives. In contrast to fleshly living, this spiritual living manifests "love, joy, peace, forbearance, kindness, goodness, faithfulness, gentleness and self-control." These attributes collectively and progressively reveal themselves in our lives as a result of us choosing "his way over our way by his power." Verse twenty-five then provides an insightful summary. Paul explains that, if the Spirit is sufficient to bring new life, we ought to follow his leading. Let's surrender to the Holy Spirit to live out the life to which we are called. Let's allow him to empower us and submit to his will in our lives to live his way for God's glory.

3 Simple Prayers

Here's the reality. If we have trusted in Jesus as our Savior, we have been made right with God. Our status has been changed from condemned to forgiven. We are a new creation with a new heart and are empowered by God himself through his Spirit to live the life to which he has called us. A new orientation of life exists for us, but this new orientation doesn't remove the internal temptation to live contrary to God's will at times; however, the presence of God's Spirit brings us power to submit our wills to God and to deny sinful fleshly desires.

Some questions may arise at this point, such as How do I do this? How can I grow in living God's way? Many answers could be given, but I encourage you to begin with prayer. I encourage you to do something right now. Go get a pen and paper and write down these three simple prayers I'm about to share with you. Put this paper somewhere you will see and remember it. Then, over the next three weeks, pray these three simple prayers daily.

1. "God, strengthen my confidence in your power."

When we grow in confidence in the power of the Holy Spirit, when we grow in confidence that, through him, we can walk in godliness, when we grow in confidence that his way brings life, we will see our lives become progressively transformed and holy. This transformation will be seen in increased victory over temptation and sin. We need to understand and believe that, through the indwelling Spirit, we have the power to live a God-glorifying life. As we grow in confidence in God's power in and through our lives, we will begin to see more clearly and experience more definitively that God's way brings greater satisfaction, greater pleasure, and greater fulfillment.

2. "God, strengthen my commitment to live in submission to your power."

A commitment to live in submission to the Spirit is a commitment to say no to sin. If we commit our will to the Spirit in resisting sin, we will be amazed at what God will do in our lives. This commitment means taking responsibility for our sin. Stop making excuses. When we sin, it's not because of an absence of power or ability; it's because of a choice we've made to do it our way versus God's way. It's a choice we've made to resist God's empowering presence in order to embrace ungodly tendencies. A commitment to live in submission to the Spirit is a commitment to stop making excuses for sin in our lives. For example:

- ❖ Quit blaming your bad boss for your lazy work habits.

- ❖ Quit blaming your irresponsibility on your video game addiction.

- ❖ Quit blaming your workload, bills, and children for your explosive temper.

- ❖ Quit blaming your diagnosis or "addiction" for your drinking or drug problem.

- ❖ Quit blaming your spouse's lack of intimacy for your Internet browsing habits.

- ❖ Quit blaming your grandfather for your promiscuity or self-destructive tendencies. Maybe your grandfather molested you. That's horrible! No child should ever have to experience such pain. At the same time, each of us is still responsible for our thoughts and actions. Take responsibility, and trust the Spirit's power to heal your emotional pain and enable you to walk in victorious strength.

I was a typical fifteen-year-old. I blamed my parents for my lot in life. I wasn't horribly rebellious, but my attitude stunk. My parents divorced when I was twelve, which left me stuck in the middle of all their fighting. One spring break, because of an invitation of a classmate, I went to a church youth camp, where the Lord convicted me of my sinful attitudes and rebellion. I had a choice. I could either take responsibility for my sin or continue to justify it by blaming my parents and making excuses. I made the decision to repent of my foul attitudes and turn to follow God's design for my life. On the way home from camp, I was in the car with my mom. We were getting on interstate I-65N in Birmingham heading home. I turned to my mother and said, "Mom, I want to ask you to forgive me. I've been blaming you for the way I've behaved and that's wrong. These are my decisions. I'm very sorry, and I want you to know that I'm going to try and live differently. I hope that you can see Jesus in and through my life." Did everything turn around at once? No, but I did quit using my parents as an excuse for my sin. I took responsibility and decided to submit to God's design for my life. Shifting the blame doesn't remove the reality of the sin. Own it, face it, and determine by God's grace to reject and overcome it. Every believer can live victoriously by the indwelling power of the Spirit of God! Say this. "I can walk in victory." Believe it. "I can walk daily in godly victory by choosing to live by the Holy Spirit's power. By God's grace, through his Spirit, I can acknowledge, repent, and overcome my sin. I can walk by God's grace for his glory."

3. "God, strengthen my contentment with godly living, regardless of circumstances."

All too often, down deep inside, we really expect comfort when we do what God wants. After all, if we quit looking at porn, we assume our spouse will become more affectionate automatically and fill that void. If we start working harder and break our lazy cycle, we expect that we will get acknowledged and get promoted. We believe that living God's way means bad things won't happen, but that is not necessarily the reality of our experience, and it certainly isn't the actual message of Jesus. Jesus, as well as the apostles, warns us that we will suffer as a result of our allegiance to him (John 15:18–20; 1 Tim. 3:12; 1 Pet. 4:1).

We must strengthen our resolve to live for God and be content with the results. We must acknowledge that we are still living in the midst of an evil world while we anticipate Jesus returning to fully establish his kingdom. Isn't this how Jesus taught us to pray? When Jesus instructed us to pray, he explained that we should pray God's "will be done, on earth as it is in heaven" (Matt. 6:10). The fact that we are to pray for God's will to be done on earth implies that godliness and spiritual wellness are not the norm here in this life. This perspective will help us not lose heart and veer off track when the results do not meet our expectations. We must remain determined that we can walk in obedience through the power of God's Spirit while accepting the earthly uncertainty of the results.

Taking It In

Paul reminded Titus of the saving life-changing power of the Holy Spirit. The Holy Spirit is the renewing force who brings new life to all of who place their faith in Jesus as Lord and Savior.

> *"But when the kindness and love of God our Savior appeared, he saved us, not because of righteous things we had done, but because of his mercy. He saved us through the washing of rebirth and renewal by the Holy Spirit, whom he poured out on us generously through Jesus Christ our Savior, so that, having been justified by his grace, we might become heirs having the hope of eternal life."*

Titus 3:4–7

Not only is the Spirit involved in giving us new life as believers, but he goes a step further. He takes up spiritual residence within us so that we are not left as orphans but sealed as children of God into the family of God (Rom. 8:9–10, 14–17). Yet the presence of the Holy Spirit in our lives is more than symbolic, and his presence is more than guaranteeing security. His presence also represents power: the power to walk God's way instead of in our old ways (Rom. 8:10–13; Gal. 5:16). If the Spirit is sufficient to save us from the condemnation of the law, as well as the penalty of sin and death, is he not also sufficient to equip us to fulfill the purposes for which we were redeemed (Gal. 5:25)?

At the beginning of this chapter, I talked about being taught that I was "a dirty, rotten, stinking, sinner." But that wasn't all I was taught. I also eventually learned that, through faith in Jesus, I'm a new creation, a saint, and a child of the King. I learned God loves me, and he has given me his very own Spirit as a special gift. As a result of this gift, I can live in victory in this world. This victorious living does not earn or secure my salvation. Rather, I seek to live victorious because God has provided me with salvation through his grace. I now want to live in a way that reflects the power of his presence in my life. Through it all, I've learned that, by surrendering to the powerful presence of the Holy Spirit in my life, I can live God's way over my way for his glory.

What if we actually sold out to this truth? What if we began to live with a renewed confidence that, by the Spirit through us, we can live for him? What if we believed that our failures were not necessary, and we refused to allow them to hold us hostage any longer? What if, by the Spirit's power, we refused to settle for defeat when we sinned but instead asked for forgiveness and then sought to live righteously? What if we were content to allow our future circumstances to be in God's hands and not allow circumstances to determine our level of obedience?

Imagine how much different our homes, workplaces, and churches would be if we stopped making excuses for sin and started living the Spirit-empowered life. The life we've always wanted can be ours, not by self-enlightenment or self-empowerment but by self-surrender to the sanctifying, indwelling, powerful presence of the Spirit of the living God! Through the Holy Spirit, we can live his way over our way by his power for his glory!

Questions for Reflection

Are there any sins you have struggled with habitually? Have you had a particular time when you felt like you were in a rut?

Have you ever experienced the conviction of the Holy Spirit? What was the circumstance? How did you know the Spirit was speaking to you?

Before reading this chapter, how would you describe the purpose of prayer? How has your understanding of prayer grown or changed in light of what you read?

How might praying "Your will be done" impact your prayer life? Would it change the way you pray? Would it impact the purpose of your prayers?

What would it look like to "live his way over our way" every day? How would it change your daily life?

CHAPTER 7
ALLEGIANCE: ALL IN FOR GOD

Overwhelmed

"Do not suppose that I have come to bring peace to the earth. I did not come to bring peace, but a sword. For I have come to turn "a man against his father, a daughter against her mother, a daughter-in-law against her mother-in-law—a man's enemies will be the members of his own household." Anyone who loves their father or mother more than me; anyone who loves their son or daughter more than me is not worthy of me. Whoever does not take their cross and follow me is not worthy of me. Whoever finds their life will lose it, and whoever loses their life for my sake will find it."

Matthew 10:34–39

We live in a society overwhelmed with choices, don't we? Television shows and movie-viewing options abound. We order water and are asked, "Would you like lemon in that?" We have more news outlets, soda combinations, mobile apps, and toothpaste options than ever before in the history of humankind. Choices surround us. Every day we live, we become more accustomed to making hundreds of choices that weren't even an option a few decades ago. Some of these choices are seemingly insignificant (such as choosing what to eat for lunch) while others have much greater consequences (such as whether to get a divorce). My wife and I (Adam), in an attempt to try and maintain our sanity and teach our kids how to make good choices, implemented a family rule regarding sports. We have a one-sport-per-season policy. "You can play one sport on one team" is the general rule we impose upon our children, and they get to pick. It's an agonizing choice for them at times, but it helps them prioritize and commit to one thing. They are learning that, while it is hard at times to commit to one thing, it is necessary. Now, as some of my children have sought to be committed, I've sat them down and explained what it takes to be exceptional and succeed. I've explained, "Do you want to know the key to excelling in anything? You have to be willing to do what others aren't. You've got to be willing to run when you don't want to. You have to be willing to shoot basketball in the rain. You have to study when you'd rather play video games. You have to be willing to go 'all in' when others want to hedge their bets."

My dear friends, the same is true for us in our relationship to Christ. If we want to experience the fullness of the relationship that Jesus extends to us, then we have to commit and be "all in!" Just like any other aspect of life, Jesus requires a commitment: a serious commitment. So, in the coming pages, let's look at Matthew 10:34–39 and examine what type of commitment Jesus requires. Let's see what it looks like to be "all in" for Jesus.

Committed

In this section of the Gospel of Matthew, Jesus was correcting some of the misperceptions that existed concerning what it meant to be his disciple. He clarifies both the personal love of God the Father and what it meant to be committed as a "Christ follower" (i.e., a Christian). It is within that context that Jesus declares, "Do not think that I have come to bring peace to the earth. I have not come to bring peace, but a sword" (Matt. 10:34).

Wait a minute! Doesn't the Bible teach that Jesus came to bring peace? After all, Zechariah, the father of one of the greatest prophets ever, John the Baptist, prophesied that, through Jesus the Messiah, God would "shine on those living in darkness and in the shadow of death, to guide our feet into the path of peace" (Luke 1:79). Later, when Jesus was born, the angels who announced his birth would collectively cry out, "Glory to God in the highest heaven, and on earth peace to those on whom his favor rests" (Luke 2:14). Furthermore, Jesus explicitly promises peace to his disciples in John 14:27 near the end of his life: "Peace I leave with you; my peace I give you. I do not give to you as the world gives. Do not let your hearts be troubled and do not be afraid." So, what's going on here? Why did Jesus assert that he came to bring strife? To grasp what is happening in Matthew 10:34, we must pause to ponder the underlying premise of Jesus' point.

We must remember that the first-century AD Jews were anticipating a Messiah who would bring "political peace and material prosperity." Jesus dispels and corrects that false notion.[27] Jesus came to reconcile us to God so that we could have peace with God externally and internally (Rom. 5:1); however, in committing our lives to Jesus, we are changing allegiance and casting our lot with a God who opposes the ways of this rebellious world. Professing faith in Jesus as the Messiah is a profession of allegiance, but it is not a profession from a neutral position. It is not like sitting objectively on the sidelines and then choosing which pick-up soccer team we want to play on. No, it's much more personal than that. It's being on one side during a war and then, in the midst of the battle, changing sides, thus betraying the cause we once served, whether we served that previous cause willingly or ignorantly. When we place our faith in Jesus as our Savior and commit our lives to him, we are spiritually delivered from the dominion of darkness. Conversely, we are commissioned into the service of Jesus as citizens of the light, serving in his kingdom and fighting for his cause as those who have been redeemed and forgiven (Col. 1:13–14). Thus, we are reconciled with God and brought into a peaceful relationship with him. At the same time, we are brought into a relationship of hostility with the world, since Jesus now takes precedence over every other relationship.

---

[27] D. A. Carson, "Matthew" in *Expositor's Bible Commentary* (Grand Rapids: Zondervan, 1984), 256.

Jesus in Matthew 10:34 contrasts peace with a sword. He explains that he came to force a decision for each of us to determine where he fits in our level of priorities. How committed to him are we? When relational values collide, which relationship will take priority? Jesus shows us that his coming brought the potential for conflict, and he now calls us to choose sides. Think of the irony here: "the believer finds peace with God but opposition from the world."[28] As a result of such a supreme commitment to Jesus, we will find an enemy in this world, and we will find division in some of our most intimate relationships. Along these lines, Jesus explains,

> "For I have come to turn "a man against his father, a daughter against her mother, a daughter-in-law against her mother-in-law—a man's enemies will be the members of his own household." Anyone who loves their father or mother more than me is not worthy of me; anyone who loves their son or daughter more than me is not worthy of me."

Matt. 10:35–37

Does this seem harsh to you? Does this seem like the Jesus we often hear about on the radio, movies, or television specials? "Hostility against Christians results not from their making themselves obnoxious but from the sad fact that, despite the peacemaking principles of [the Bible], sometimes the gospel so alienates unbelievers that they lash out against those who would love them for Christ's sake."[29] When our allegiance is supremely to Christ, it forces us to respond accordingly, even at times over and above those we love. The conflict Jesus brings is not conflict as a result of personality or socio-political differences. It is conflict that arises out of our commitment to him as our Lord.

Following Jesus comes at a significant cost. That is why Jesus challenges us to consider the personal cost involved and commit to

[28]Grant R. Osborne, *Matthew* (Grand Rapids: Zondervan, 2010), 404.
[29]Craig Blomberg, *Matthew*, vol. 22, NAC (Nashville: B&H, 1992), 180.

him supremely, not just above every other relationship but even above our own desires and life. Then he continues, "Whoever does not take up their cross and follow me is not worthy of me" (Matt. 10:38). The cross was a humiliating form of execution. The cross was a cruel cursed instrument of torture often used by the Roman Empire. Yet, oddly enough, Jesus used that symbol to describe the demands of following him. He says, "Here is what allegiance to me looks like. Look to the cross. You must die to self!" While at first glance this may seem terribly demanding, take a moment and look at the consequence of not being "all in." Jesus continue, "Whoever finds their life will lose it, and whoever loses their life for my sake will find it" (Matt, 10:39). Here Jesus explains the terrible consequences for those who are unwilling to give up their life and surrender themselves to him. They regrettably do not understand all that is at stake for them. While they may think that they are preserving their own lives, in actuality, they are losing true life. Jesus essentially declares, "If you want true life, then you must sacrifice your worldly life to me. True life is not found in this sinful temporal life, but only in me."

Today, Jesus still demands our ultimate allegiance. Jesus demands that we go "all in." The good news that Jesus brings is that he offers us eternal life. Jesus offers us atonement from sin. Jesus offers us salvation, forgiveness, and freedom. Jesus offers us an inheritance in heaven that will never perish or diminish. In return, Jesus demands complete allegiance. He demands we surrender our lives to him. Jesus demands we give up our futile pursuit of life and purpose apart from him. So, are we ready to go "all in?" Below are four observations built upon and related to the text we just discussed from Matthew 10. Let's walk through the observations and dig down a little deeper concerning the implications of our "all in" commitment to Jesus.

Making It Count

1. I am to strive for peace, but not at the expense of my allegiance to Christ.

Throughout the New Testament, disciples of Jesus are called to try and live in peace with others. Here are a few examples:

"Blessed are the peacemakers, for they will be called children of God."

Matthew 5:9

"If it is possible, as far as it depends on you, live at peace with everyone."

Romans 12:18

"Make every effort to live in peace with everyone and to be holy; without holiness no one will see the Lord."

Hebrews 12:14

Matthew talks about peace in his account of Jesus' life when recalling the sermon Jesus preached one time on a mountainside. Jesus revealed there that we are to strive for peace to the point that we don't demand things back when they are borrowed, we allow people to take advantage of us, and we turn the other cheek when insulted (Matt. 5:38–42). Our lives should be marked by peaceful living; however, the text we examined before (Matt. 10:34–39) reveals a gospel-centered division that is created out of our unrelenting devotion to Jesus. So, Matthew is not talking about creating a scene and causing a fight with your boss when he tells you that you can't have a copy of the 10 commandments on the wall of your office. Submit to your boss as the authority God has over you (Rom. 13:1–7; 1 Pet. 2:11–17). Just take them down if he asks you. Such a request is not impacting your allegiance to Jesus. Your boss is not asking you to sin. If your boss owns or pays the rent for the office space in which you work, then he or she has the authority to choose how it is decorated. Furthermore, this submission to Jesus also means that we are prohibited from slandering them all over social media. Doing so only does more damage to our witness. What Jesus is asking of us is that when people force us to choose in our hearts an allegiance to Jesus or an allegiance to any other relationship, we choose Jesus. When such a situation arises whereby we are asked to sin against, dismiss, or downplay our relationship with Jesus, we choose Jesus over that other relationship. For example:

❖ If we are asked to "cook the books" at work or transfer inventory records for double counts so that things look better than they are, we don't obey. We stand firm on our conviction that lying is wrong and seek to be a person of integrity in obedience to Jesus regardless of the cost.

❖ When we are told to take sales clients to strip clubs and go out drinking to close the deal, we refuse. We don't have to make a scene about it, we just stand firm in our conviction. We commit first to Jesus and ask that the assignment is given to someone else or ask for the freedom to close the deal through godly and ordinary means.

❖ When we are told that we must begin working Sunday mornings on a regular basis, then we have to decide whether can still be a faithful, active member of a local body of believers. If we can't, if working on Sunday means we have to stop worshipping and ministering in our local church, then it means we will have to decline the request or find another job.

2. Devotion to family is a Christian responsibility, but it does not override my devotion to Jesus.

There may be times in our Christian experience when we will have to decide between our commitment to our biological family and our commitment to Jesus. I've heard of couples with children called by God to go to the mission field who were torn with uncertainty because of their parents. Their parents were hurt and angry because this beautiful couple would dare to take their grandbabies off to a foreign country. In one such case, the parents even threatened to write them out of the will. While the couple chose to obey their Savior, it was a gut-wrenching decision. Such an example is why we have to choose now to cherish Jesus over riches and over all other relationships. This concept applies to marriage as well. When spouses do not share the same commitment to Jesus, it creates tension. I've seen wives who husbands forbid them from going to church. These women were forced to choose between obeying the command to gather faithfully with believers in the worship of the Lord or obey and honor their husbands (Heb. 10:24–25; 1 Pet. 3:1–6).

We will experience a tension between our relationship with our family or friends and our relationship with Jesus anytime our devotion to him and his word collide with irreconcilable worldly values and demands. For example, let's say we are at a family gathering where there is intoxication, profanity, gossiping, dirty jokes, or racial slurs. Because of our commitment to Jesus, we are committed to sobriety, clean talk, and loving others. As a result, our choice to honor Jesus does not allow us to participate in such behavior. While we do not necessarily have to leave the family party, our lack of active participation and approval will lessen the intimacy we experience with our family.

John G. Fee was a minister and educator in Berea, Kentucky, who fought for the abolishment of slavery in the 1800s. His journal highlights the familial tensions that arise when one is forced to choose between their allegiance to Jesus and their family. Reverend Fee was convinced of the horrors of slavery, having seen them first-hand as the son of a slave owner. He reflected on his conviction of the evil of slavery and the dignity deserved for every human life in his journal.

> *Here, let me say, the torture of the body is terribly cruel, and yet it is the smallest part of the crime of human slavery. I have seen women tied to a tree or a timber and whipped with cow-hides on their bare bodies until their shrieks would seem to rend the very heavens. I have seen a man, a father, guilty only of the crime of absenting himself from*

work for a day and two nights, on his return home whipped with a cow-hide on his bare flesh until his blood ran to his heels. Thousands of slaves have been whipped and beaten to death even for trivial offenses, as that of a slave in a county adjoining to this, whipped to death for going, in the hour of night, to see his wife, in violation of the master's commands. Yet this torture of the body was the least part of the agony of slavery. The acme of the crime was on the soul. The crushing of human hearts, sundering the ties of husband and wife, parent and child, shrouding all of manhood in the long night of despair, - the crime was on the soul! The agony of our Lord in Gethsemane was that of the soul, not that of the body.

The youth of this generation cannot comprehend the enormity of human slavery, - the effect of it upon society, - how it blunted the sensibilities, outraged every element of justice, fostered licentiousness, violence and crime of almost every description. And yet those who practiced and sustained this iniquity, often occupied commanding positions both in church and state! And here I wish to say, that the same misrepresentation of Christianity is seen in those who maintain the spirit and practice of caste, - a relic of the barbarism of slavery. To crush by slight or invidious conduct, in church or in civil society, any man or woman of merit, is as truly oppressive and wicked as slavery itself. I speak of conduct toward meritorious persons. As to what our conduct should be we need only to ask what our Lord, our great Exampler, would do were he here in flesh.[30]

Reverend Fee, along with others, built a church in which all people would be welcome and free to worship as children made in the image of God. Above the door, a white marble slab was placed

---

[30]John G. Fee, *The Autobiography of John G. Fee, Berea, Kentucky* (Chicago: National Christian Assocation, 1891), 69–71. A digital version was accessed at http://docsouth.unc.edu/fpn/fee/fee.html on 17 Feb 2017.

with the inscription "Free Church of Christ," to openly and boldly signify that this church was Jesus' church, non-denominational, and welcoming of anyone.[31] After building this church, it came to Fee's attention that a slave named Julett under his father's care was going to be sold. Fee, determined to redeem Julett and set her free, mounted his horse, rode the twenty-five miles to his father's house, and spent the night. He then recorded in his journal:

> In the morning of the next day I sought an opportunity when my father was alone, and having learned that he would sell, asked what he would take for Julett. He fixed his price. I said: "Will you sell her to me if I bring to you the money?" He said yes. I immediately rode to Germantown and borrowed the requisite amount of money by mortgaging my remaining tract of land for the payment. Whilst there I executed a bill of sale, so that without delay my father could sign it, before he even returned from the field at noon. I tendered to him the money and the bill of sale. He signed the bill of sale, and took the money. I immediately went to "Add," the husband of Julett, and told him I had bought Julett and should immediately secure by law her freedom. I said to him: "I would gladly redeem you but I have not the means." He replied: "I am glad you can free her; I can take care of myself better than she can." I went to the house, wrote a perpetual pass for the woman, gave it to her, and said, "You are a free woman; be in bondage to no man." Tears of gratitude ran down her sable cheeks. I then told her that at the first county-court day I would take her to the clerk's office, where her height could be taken and she be otherwise described, and a record of her freedom made. This was just before the amendment to the State Constitution that forbade emancipation in the State. At noon my father came in and told my mother of the transaction. My mother was displeased, - did not want to spare the woman from certain work for which she was

---

[31]Ibid., 59.

fitted. My father came to me and requested that I cancel the contract and give up the bill of sale. I said to him, "Here is my horse, and I have a house and lot in Lewis County; I will give them to you if you so desire; but to sell a human being I may not." He became very angry and went to the freed woman and said to her, "When you leave this house never put your foot on my farm again, for I do not intend to have a free nigger on my farm." The woman, the wife and mother, came to me and said, "Master says if I leave here I shall never come back again; I cannot leave my children; I would rather go back into slavery." I said, ["]I have done what I regarded as my duty. To now put you back into slavery, I cannot. We must simply abide the consequences.["] The woman was in deep distress and helpless as a child. Although I had my horse and was ready to ride, I felt I could not leave the helpless one until a way of relief should open. After a time Julett came to me and said, "As long as mistress shall live I can stand it; I would rather stay." I said, "You are a free woman and must make your own decision. If my father will furnish to you a home, and clothe and feed you, and you shall choose as a free woman to stay, all well; but to sell you back into slavery, I cannot." To this proposition to furnish a home to the freed woman my father agreed. There was now a home for the freed woman, and this with her husband and children and grand-children.

That day of agony was over and eventide had come. I spent the night. The next morning just as I was about starting back to my home, my father said to me, "Julett is here on my premises, and I will sell her before sundown if I can." I turned to him and said, "Father, I am now that woman's only guardian. Her husband cannot protect her, - I only can. I must do as I would be done by; and though it is hard for me to now say to you what I intended to say, yet if you sell that woman, I will prosecute you for so doing, as sure as you are a man." I saw the peril of the defenseless woman. I would gladly have cast from me the cup of a further contest, but I saw that to leave her, though now a free woman, was not the end of obligation. I felt forcibly the applicability of the words, "Cursed be he that doeth the work of the Lord negligently, and cursed be he that keepeth back the sword from blood." Jer. 48:10. I mounted my horse and rode twelve miles where I could get legal counsel, - counsel on which I could rely. I found that if I left the woman on my father's premises without any public record of her having been sold, the fact of her being then on his premises would be regarded as "prima facie" evidence that she was his property and that he could sell her. I also found that in as much as he had sold her to me, I could, by law, compel him to do that which was just and right, - make a record of the fact of sale. I rode back twelve miles, told my father what was his legal obligation, and asked him to conform to it. He said he would not. I then said to him, "It will be a hard trial for me to arraign my father in a civil court, for neglect of justice to a helpless woman, and also for a plain violation of law; but I will do so, as sure as you are a man, if you do not make the required record of sale." After hesitancy and delay he made the record. These were hours of distress to me, to my father, to my mother, and to the ransomed woman; but the only way to ultimate peace, was to hold on rigidly to the right; though in so doing I had, in the Gospel sense, to leave father, mother, brother, sisters, houses, lands, - all, for Christ's sake. I was conscious that no other motive impelled me.

The legal process ended, the woman was then secure, and in a home, for the time being, with her husband and children. Not long after this my mother died. The services of the freed woman were the more needed where she then was. To her were born, into freedom, three more children. About this time her husband, through a friend, found the

record of the time of his bond service. He, by legal process,
secured his freedom and recovered several hundred dollars,
as compensation for services rendered beyond the time he
should have enjoyed his liberty.[32]

Reverend Fee was compelled not simply by personal feelings of compassion but by his commitment to Jesus his Lord. He was not simply an advocate for social justice. He was not simply moved by societal reforms and a desire to see a better nation. No, he was compelled by the plain teaching of Jesus and his personal responsibility to live in obedience to him above all else. Fee chose Jesus over his family.

3. If I stand with Jesus, I will have to choose him over some other relationships.

Supreme allegiance to Jesus goes beyond our familial relationships and principally applies to every relationship we encounter. When we are asked to compromise our commitment to biblical purity on a date or on social media, do we give in so that we don't risk losing this person, or do we stay faithful to Jesus? We can't do both. Our actions declare our allegiance. When we are asked to push further into immodesty and remove more clothing for modeling opportunities, who will we honor and what desires will we allow to determine our choices? These choices are not always about doing something that is clearly wrong, sometimes those around us might seek to pressure us, intentionally or unintentionally, to quit doing something that is right just because our presence is convicting to them. We may even find ourselves in a position in which professing Christians pressure us to choose them over our commitment to Jesus. I remember being in school and having some close friends of mine go out to party. These friends were all professing believers, and their partying wasn't necessarily ungodly. When I heard they went without me, being a little hurt, I asked why I wasn't invited. The response shocked me. I was told that I talked about Jesus too much and they didn't want to hear that

---

[32]Ibid., 61–66.

stuff that night. Such a statement presents a tension in our lives when we realize our relationship with Jesus is causing our relationship with friends to suffer. In those moments, we have a choice to make. To whom are we ultimately committed: ourselves, others, or Jesus?

4. Jesus wants every part of my life, not just my Sunday mornings and quiet times.

Christianity is simply one part of life for far too many "professing" believers, yet this segmented approach is far from the biblical approach of following Jesus. Jesus isn't to be a part of our lives; Jesus is to be the center of our lives. Allegiance to Jesus should impact and direct every aspect of our lives. Following Jesus is about worshipping Jesus, and unfortunately, we've often relegated worship to our Sunday morning "worship services" and "quiet times." Consequently, we tend to think of these moments as spending time with God, and then we walk away to live our lives on our own. Such a mindset is false, disingenuous, and dangerous. Jesus is with us throughout our day. Sunday mornings and selected times of private Bible reading and prayer are simply moments in which we focus more intently on our walk with God. As we leave from those times, we leave with Jesus. As we live our lives, we are to live in allegiance to and in worship of Jesus. We do not simply follow him; we worship him as indicated by the affections of our heart, the words of our mouth, the thoughts of our mind, and the actions of our life. He is with us in all things at all times. Understanding this reality should help us in actualizing the truth that Jesus came not only to redeem us from our sin so that we can spend eternity with him in heaven but also to redeem the entirety of our lives on this planet. Jesus calls all his children of faith to surrender their lives over to him completely. He calls us to die to our self-driven pursuits and yield to his good and perfect will. In return, he gives us so much more than we could have hoped for on our own.

Are You All In?

The term "all in" is a poker term. A player states that he or she is "all in" after they have read their cards, have read the "tells" of their opponents, and have calculated that the chances of winning big are worth risking all they have on the table. It is at that moment that they shove all of their chips, sometimes hundreds of thousands of dollars, into the center of the table and definitively state, "I'm all in." When they do that, there is no going back, there are no do-overs, no mulligans, it's the end of the line for them because for them "the chips are down," literally. Being "all in" is not some kind of "cool" saying; it's a definitive, non-negotiable action.

Why are people willing to go "all in" on anything? It's because they believe it's worth it. They believe the risk is worth the reward. Think about it. Why do people commit to running marathons? Why do people commit to building a house? Why do people commit to marriage? Why do people commit to run into a burning building in hopes of saving one life? It's because to them it's worth it! Do you believe going "all in" for Jesus is worth it?

Regrettably, Christianity is often proposed to potential converts in a way sometimes referred to as "easy believism." In other words, people are told they can have all the benefits of Jesus with absolutely no reference to the sacrifices Jesus demands as found in the Gospel of Matthew. They want Jesus without any of the sacrifice. People are told they can believe in Jesus by only acknowledging him without expressing genuine faith and repentance. People are told that if they accept Jesus' love, they will have eternal life, regardless of the true allegiance of their hearts or the indications of their lives. Such a message is a false gospel. It's not good news; it's damning news because it deceitfully convinces people that they are safe when in fact they are in danger. How ironic it is that many people are fooled into thinking that there is no sacrifice involved in following someone that the world literally executed on a Roman cross. The cost of following Jesus is our lives, but the cost of rejecting Jesus is our souls. Considering such a cost is an important part of the Christian life (Luke 14:28–33). In an attempt to ensure potential converts in South Asia were considering the real cost of following Jesus, it was reported that some professing converts were presented seven questions they must answer before being baptized.

1. Are you willing to leave home and lose the blessing of your father?

2. Are you willing to lose your job?

3. Are you willing to go to the village and those who persecute you, forgive them, and share the love of Christ with them?

4. Are you willing to give an offering to the Lord?

5. Are you willing to be beaten rather than deny your faith?

6. Are you willing to go to prison?

7. Are you willing to die for Jesus?[33]

While I don't know if these questions were ever actually asked, the article highlighted an important truth. Following Jesus requires our ultimate allegiance. Following Jesus requires us to go "all in."

The question is "Are we all in?" Karen Watson was. She was murdered in 2004 while serving as a missionary in Iraq. She gave the ultimate price to follow her Savior and tell others about him, but it was a price she was willing to pay. She left behind a sealed letter only to be opened in the event of her death. Part of the letter read,

> When God calls, there are no regrets. I tried to share my heart with you as much as possible, my heart for the nations. I wasn't called to a place. I was called to Him, to glory. To obey was my objective. To suffer was expected. His glory was my reward. His glory is my reward...Care more than some think is wise, risk more than some think is safe, dream more than some think is practical and expect

---

[33]"7 Questions for New Converts in an Asian Country," *Leadership* 33 (2012): 60.

more than some think is possible. I was called not to comfort or success but to obedience.[34]

Is Jesus your most important relationship? Have you made the choice to go "all in" for and with him? Putting Jesus first is not only about honoring him above all other relationships but also about honoring him before yourself. Jesus deserves and demands our ultimate allegiance. That's part of what it means to be his follower.

Questions for Reflection

What does it look like to go all in for Jesus? What other allegiances often draw us away?

Why does Jesus demand that his followers "lose their life" for his sake? What does it mean to die to self?

Do you ever struggle to live at peace with others? What circumstances make this most difficult? When should we choose obedience to God over unity?

Have you ever felt the tension between following Christ and pleasing your own family? What were the circumstances and how did you respond?

Is there any act of obedience you are struggling with today? How can others pray for you and with you? Do you need accountability, encouragement, or help?

---

[34] David Roach, "Mohler: Slain missionaries spotlight need for worldwide Gospel proclamation," *Southern News* [on-line]; accessed 24 February 2017; http://news.sbts.edu/2004/04/01/mohler-slain-missionaries-spotlight-need-for-worldwide-gospel-proclamation/; Internet.

CHAPTER 8
AMBASSADORSHIP: SENT BY GOD

Off Course

Twenty twelve- and thirteen-year-old boys approached a rickety old scale to weigh-in. It was football, and it was game day. In Alabama in the 1980s, most of the community football leagues were broken down into weight divisions. I'd (Adam) been crushing people in practice. It felt good. I played defensive end, and I couldn't wait for the game to start. Our team stood on the sideline, hitting each other on the pads to get pumped for the game. Finally, the game started, and for the first time in my life, I was a star. I had multiple sacks and unassisted tackles. I was so dominant that the other team was forced to run or pass away from me most of the game. I'd never felt so good. It was amazing. I was named the player of the game, the player of the week, and was called out during the next practice as an example. This was my year! At least, it was my year until later in that week. The coach had our team doing fumble drills, where he would toss the football about ten yards and have two people race to see who could jump on the ball first. During the drill, I tripped. Everyone heard the crack. My arm was suddenly at an odd seventy-degree angle with a bad break. One trip to the emergency room and one cast later, my little league football career was over. I came to a few more practices, but I just didn't understand my role anymore. I felt so lost. I felt purposeless.

Have you ever felt lost? Have you ever wondered what your purpose is? Maybe you have had such a dark past that you wonder if you are useful anymore. Can you recover from such mistakes? Maybe you heard the stirring message of God's love and gave your life to Jesus. You walked the aisle and "accepted" him. The minister prayed with and congratulated you. Then the service ended, everyone left, and you continued life as usual. Nothing really changed in your mind but your final destination. Maybe you sat in a stirring service where you sensed God calling you into ministry. You took a position at a church, but that didn't really work out. You are now married with kids and a regular job. What are you supposed to do? Who are you now? Did you miss God's plan? Did God mess up? The point is that there are all types of circumstances in which we might wonder "What's my role on God's team?" or "What assignment does God want me to do?" All too often we base our worth on our abilities and our vocation, yet God declares that our worth is not in who we are but whose we are. For all of us who belong to Jesus, he has a purposeful role for us on his team. So, let's walk through 2 Corinthians 5:17–21 and look at that role.

Commissioned

Paul wrote to bring encouragement and correction to the church in Corinth. His directions for them are still instructive for us today and just as applicable as they were those many years ago. He wrote, "Therefore, if anyone is in Christ, the new creation has come: The old has gone, the new is here!" (2 Cor. 5:17). God is in the saving business, and the greatest salvation anyone needs is spiritual. God is a holy God, and we as sinners stand on our own condemned before him. Our only hope is mercy and grace. That is why God sent his Son Jesus to live on our behalf, die in our place, and rise for our victory. When we trust completely in him, when we believe in Jesus as the one who attained our salvation, we are placed "in Christ" as a "new creation." Being in Christ means we as "Christians see the world in a new way and become new when [we] are joined to Christ."[35] The old way of life, the old identity, and the old order have passed. Something new is happening in, through, and around those who are in Christ. The phrase "in Christ" also reveals several other truths. It reveals that we belong to (are united with) Jesus. It

---

[35]David E. Garland, *2 Corinthians*, vol. 29, NAC (Nashville: B&H, 1999), 287.

reiterates that we are to now live in Jesus' power, not our own, and that we are now part of a believing community with others who are joined together in Jesus.[36]

All this "newness," all this grace, is a gift from Almighty God, who renewed us for a purpose. God has a master plan, and it includes us. Look closely at what Paul also wrote. "All this is from God, who reconciled us to himself through Christ and *gave us the ministry of reconciliation*: that God was reconciling the world to himself in Christ, not counting people's sins against them. And he has *committed to us the message of reconciliation*. We are therefore Christ's ambassadors..." (2 Cor. 5:18–20a).[37] So what is God's master plan? What is God's plan for reaching the world? What is God's plan for reaching those in the dark native jungles on distant continents? What is God's plan for reaching those in nations closed to the gospel? What is God's plan for reaching our neighbors and co-workers? It's us! It's me! It's you! It's all who are now in Christ. We are God's master plan. When we placed our faith in Jesus, we changed our citizenship and became ambassadors on foreign soil. And what is an ambassador? An ambassador is someone commissioned by a greater authority to go as a representative of that authority. That's who we are. We are ambassadors of and for the Lord Jesus Christ. We were made new creations for this very purpose.

It was the summer of 1999, and I was working at an auto-paint store where we mixed, sold, and delivered paint. Across the street was a body shop. One of their employees regularly came in to hang out and talk. I didn't know who he was or what he did over there, just that he stopped by often and visited. One day, as he and I were talking, I asked him what he did. His response still captivates me and illustrates Paul's point well. He lowered his voice and said, "I'm an evangelist disguised as a painter." He proceeded to talk about how he was on mission for Jesus to let others know about him. His

---

[36]Ibid., 286.
[37]Emphasis added.

responsibility was to represent Jesus in everything he did and tell others about the wonderful name of Jesus. He got it! He understood his calling on a level few of us ever do. He understood what it meant to be an ambassador of Christ.

Representatives

Four and a half months after getting married, I was sent to Japan by the United States Marine Corps. Not long before I arrived in Japan, three military personnel had attacked a young Japanese lady. Tensions were high, and we were constantly reminded that when we were in town, we represented more than ourselves. We represented the United States of America. It reminded me of a story George Shultz told Brian Lamb on C-Span's *Booknotes* on June 27, 1993. Shultz was Secretary of State during the Regan presidency. When ambassadors met with him, he would occasionally test them. "You have to go over the globe," he would say, "and prove to me that you can identify your country." The appointed ambassador would go over, spin the globe, and put their finger on the country to which he or she was commissioned. When an old friend and former Senate Majority Leader Mike Mansfield, who at the time was the ambassador to Japan, was visiting, Secretary Shultz put him to the test. This time, however, Ambassador Mansfield spun the globe and put his finger on the United States. He said, "That's my country." That experience changed Secretary Shultz. From then on, he told what Ambassador Mansfield said "to all the ambassadors going out. 'Never forget you're over there in that country, but your country is the United States. You're there to represent us.'"[38]

Obstacles become Opportunities

That's our job. That's our role on God's team! We are all ambassadors representing our King. We have the privilege of representing Jesus and delivering his message throughout the

---

[38]"George Shultz: Turmoil and Triumph: My Years as Secretary of State," *Booknotes*, accessed July 7, 2014, http://www.booknotes.org/FullPage.aspx?SID=44051-1.

world! But let's be honest. Understanding this tremendous privilege of ambassadorship provides a clear path of calling, but it does not remove all of our issues. We like the idea of an ambassadorship to France. We just don't want to be an ambassador to Libya. Why? Because one post seems safer, more enjoyable, and more prestigious. We don't necessarily mind serving, but comparatively, we want to serve in more comfortable and glamorous places. Moreover, we certainly don't want to go and serve, only to feel taken advantage of or persecuted for our service. If we were to serve as an ambassador, we would want some reasonable assurances, some reasonable protections, and some reasonable accommodations. That's understandable, and as Christians, God promises those things as well, just not in this world. The deal is that we serve as his ambassador for his purposes in this life, regardless of how uncomfortable it may be, while in the kingdom to come we have the guarantee of safety, security, privilege, and pleasure. Truthfully, no one likes to suffer, and all too often, we view suffering as something happening only to those out of God's will. That's simply not the case. The Bible is full of people who suffered as faithful servants of God (Heb. 11:35–38). Sometimes God calls us to serve in suffering as ambassadors for his redemptive purposes. It is often in the midst of suffering that our testimony is most credible. Think about it. We often respect those who stand firm for their convictions in the face of opposition; consequently, it should be no different for our faith in and love for God. To hold fast in the face of suffering is to preach through a megaphone! It amplifies what we are saying by communicating that what we know to be true is more important than our comfort or safety. Consider these life situations and the credibility they can bring to your faith. Have you received a bad medical report? God has given you a platform of ambassadorship. God has provided you with an audience that might not listen otherwise. Have you been divorced? Use that to reach people who those of us who aren't divorced can't. Use your experience to promote the greatness and glory of God in a way those who haven't experienced your difficulty might not be able to. Have you lost a child? There is possibly no worse pain. No parent should have such a horrific experience; nevertheless, some do suffer this great tragedy. And, if you are an ambassador of Christ who has suffered such loss, you have an experience from which you can identify with sorrow on a level few can comprehend. You have an opportunity to minister and speak uniquely into the lives of others who have also experienced terrible loss. Here is one last thought concerning how this point of suffering creates a platform. How did God provide reconciliation to the world? By sending Jesus the Son as an ambassador on his behalf, right? And what was the way in which Jesus was used? He was crucified for our sins. My point? If Christ, as our example of proclaiming God's plan to the world, did so in the midst of suffering, why do we believe that we should be exempt from it? Along these lines, Peter admonishes his audience, "Dear friends, do not be surprised at the fiery ordeal that has come on you to test you, as though something strange were happening to you. But rejoice inasmuch as you participate in the sufferings of Christ, so that you may be overjoyed when his glory is revealed" (1 Pet. 4:12–13).

Message Couriers

Paul writes that we are ambassadors on behalf of Jesus Christ, and as ambassadors, it is "as though God were making his appeal through us" (2 Cor. 5:20b). As we go forth representing Jesus, we do so as God's agents of proclamation. Our ambassadorship is not simply living as Jesus' representative in the world, but it is also proclaiming the same message of God that Jesus proclaimed. We are God's plan for proclaiming his message to the world. We have the privilege of being the mouthpiece of God. How amazing is that? If I send my middle daughter Meagan to tell my other children that it is time to clean up, she is my representative delivering my message. Consequently, my other children will be held accountable for the message I send through her. This responsibility to deliver an important message faithfully is precisely what Paul is emphasizing in this passage. A verbal witness is involved here. Do you see it? Regrettably, the lack of a verbal proclamation of the gospel is a central weakness of many of the evangelistic methods that are advocated these days. They do not emphasize the biblical necessity of verbally presenting others with the gospel message. The Bible is clear regarding the essential nature of a verbal witness (Rom. 10:14). Relational evangelism is relating to others through service, friendship, or lifestyle *for the intended purpose* of the Lord opening an opportunity to show and share God's love in the gospel.[39] If the intended purpose is not to see a door opened to verbally share the gospel, it is not evangelism. We can call it service, friendship, gospel living, etc., but we dare not say that we have been ambassadors spreading the gospel. Let's think about it this way. If we only live a godly life, serve in selfless ways, or develop genuine friendships without any explanation, people will not necessarily connect our faith with Jesus. People will not inherently understand that Jesus is the object of our faith and the motivation for living righteously as a result of grace (Eph. 2:10). People will not know that Jesus is "the way and the truth and the life" (John 14:6). Without a verbal witness, people will have no necessary grid from which to attribute our actions to the good news of Jesus. Without such an explanation, people may just as easily attribute our "good works" to Buddha, Muhammad, Karma, or (more than likely) the idea that we are just "good people." In the end, without a verbal witness, we run the considerable risk of communicating the false gospel of moralism, which teaches those who can't be good that if they somehow could be good they would go to heaven.[40] Without an articulation of the gospel, people will never understand Jesus as the object of faith, the cleanser of our sins, and the continual provider of his grace that compels us to live righteously for him (Eph. 2:10).

Exemplifying the reality that we are called to be vocal ambassadors, Paul continues, "We implore you on Christ's behalf:

---

[39]Dave Earley and David Wheeler, *Evangelism Is...* (Nashville: B&H, 2010), 151, 185.

[40]By "good" here, I mean "righteous." People can commit decent or "good" acts regardless of their faith persuasion; however, people cannot commit a righteous act before God in their present fallen state apart from the sanctifying and enabling work of God in their lives.

Be reconciled to God. God made him who had no sin to be sin for us, so that in him we might become the righteousness of God" (2 Cor. 5:20c–21). After acknowledging the necessity of the verbal witness, Paul models what ambassadors do by verbally communicating God's message of reconciliation. Paul begs those who have yet to embrace by faith the transforming grace of God to be reconciled to God through the atoning work of Jesus. Paul demonstrates for us how a vocal ambassadorship should be a natural byproduct of a life that has experienced the love of God and a life that loves others. Doesn't that make sense? After all, if we believe this message of hope is true for us, shouldn't it move us to share it with others? I understand that this example has been used a lot, but the quote by Penn Jillette, of the magician duo Penn and Teller, asks this question, "How much do you have to hate someone not to proselytize?"[41] This challenge comes from someone who doesn't believe in God but understands the natural correlation between genuine faith and love and the verbal sharing of that faith. Paul proudly proclaimed God's message of reconciliation, and so should we.

"To Chance Your Arm"

Every Christian has a purpose. Every Christian has a calling. Every Christian has been commissioned to a vocal ambassadorship. In light of this calling we share, I encourage us to examine and embrace three truths.

The first truth is: we have purpose in this life. We are not called to plod through life surviving in anticipation of heaven. We are not earthly sojourners just biding our time. No. That's not the biblical picture of the Christian life. We are not called just to wait for "the sweet by and by." God wants to use us now. God has a purpose for us so long as we are on this earth. God has commissioned us to be his vocal ambassadors so that, through us, those who do not have a

---

[41]Rich Maurer, "Not proselytize," YouTube video, 00:53, posted November 13, 2009, accessed April 7, 2017, http://www.youtube.com/watch?v=owZc3Xq8obk#t=34.

relationship with God might be made right with God by believing in the gospel.

While most of us as Christians readily acknowledge this truth, we seem hesitant to act upon it. The idea of talking to someone about God is often terrifying for irrational reasons. Now, to be fair, many of our brothers and sisters around the world are regularly put at risk because of their faith. Thousands lose their lives each year because of their boldness to share Jesus verbally. Yet they are not the ones who are hesitant to embrace their calling as God's ambassadors. More often than not, it seems believers in nations that allow for considerable freedom of religious expression are some of the most afraid to share their faith. Why? What is there to lose? Let's review some of the more likely areas in which we will experience loss. For most, the most significant risk of loss is social standing. Sharing God's word with others can make people feel awkward, creating social tension. That's it. That's the big risk; however, most people will not feel awkward about the conversation if we are not awkward. If we are kind in our approach, if we stop when they ask us to, and if we are consistent in living what we believe, most people will readily listen to us. What about friendships? Sharing God's message may end up costing some of us a friendship. The realization by our friends that we have competing worldviews and we think they are lost in sin may cause the other person to pull back, creating distance in the once-close relationship. The continued social pressure to keep our religious views private may create problems in the workplace for those who are faithful in living and sharing their faith. These workplace difficulties should not be the result of us violating reasonable company policies such as not talking about religion when active in the job. However, talking about our faith on breaks is appropriate; nevertheless, some of us will experience a backlash for doing that which is perfectly within our rights. Such repercussions are real, but in the grand scheme of things, such sacrifices are small in comparison to what many of our global brothers and sisters are experiencing in nations hostile to all things Christian. Finally, for a select few of us, speaking out as God's representative may cost us some family relationships, especially if we have a family member committed to a different religion. We must not allow our level of faithfulness to be hampered by our fears of potential loses. We must honestly acknowledge that, for the vast majority of us, the risk is minimal, if not non-existent. Nevertheless, a risk still exists, and the risk is real to each of us. We need the courage by God's grace in the midst of those moments to "chance our arm." What does that mean? To "chance one's arm" is an old Irish expression that comes from a family feud. Here's the story.

> *In 1492 two Irish families, the Butlers of Ormonde and the FitzGeralds of Kildare, were involved in a bitter feud. This disagreement centred around the position of Lord Deputy. Both families wanted one of their own to hold the position. In 1492 this tension broke into outright warfare and a small skirmish occurred between the two families just outside the city walls. The Butlers, realising that the fighting was getting out of control, took refuge in the Chapter House of Saint Patrick's Cathedral. The FitzGeralds followed them into the Cathedral and asked them to come out and make peace. The Butlers, afraid that if they did so they would be slaughtered, refused. As a gesture of good faith the head of the Kildare family, Gerald FitzGerald, ordered that a hole be cut in the door. He then thrust his arm through the door and offered his hand in peace to those on the other side. Upon seeing that FitzGerald was willing to risk his arm by putting it through the door the Butlers reasoned that he was serious in his intention. They shook hands through the door, the Butlers emerged from the Chapter House and the two families made peace. Today this door is known as the "Door of Reconciliation" and is on display in the Cathedral's north transept. This story also lives on in a famous expression in Ireland "To chance your arm."[42]*

---

[42]"The Door of Reconciliation," May 26, 2016, accessed April 7, 2017: https://www.stpatrickscathedral.ie/the-door-of-reconciliation/. See also, St.

So, in order to see others reconciled with God, would we be willing to take a little risk. It may be hard, but the eternal destiny of one's soul is worth our potential sacrifices.

The second truth is: we are to expect God to be working. We should expect God through his Spirit to be moving in the lives of the very people we are called to interact as ambassadors. Do we? Unfortunately, we prematurely expect people to be resistant to our efforts. We expect people to be offended, annoyed, or inconvenienced. We expect to fail. I remember being in the tenth grade. I had just survived a horrific car accident that should have taken my life. I was new to my school, so few people were aware of what had happened. I was emotionally broken and spiritual searching on the inside, despite appearing as if everything was okay on the outside. Well, one November day, I was sitting in class when a boy I hardly knew walked up to me and asked if I would like to go to church with him sometime. I was a little surprised because I certainly wasn't expecting such an invitation at school that day. Regardless, I told him, "Sure, I'd love to." I still remember his response. He looked disappointed, slumped his shoulders a little, and mumbled, "I understand." He then turned and began to walk away. I jumped up, tugged his arm, and said, "No, I really would like to go to church with you." The next Sunday, he and his family came by and picked me up for church. God eventually used that church to stir a passion in my heart for the things of God and put me on a path to serve him in vocational ministry. I also met the woman who eventually became my wife at this church. I sometimes wonder where I would be if he hadn't simple reached out to me and risked a little social awkwardness. But, to the point we are making here, I also sometimes wonder what he thought I initially said when I responded to his invitation. This young man expected to fail. He expected rejection. He didn't expect to encounter someone in whom God was already working. I find that many of us are like this young

---

Patrick's Cathedral Dublin, "St Patricks Cathedral Dublin - Door of Reconciliation," YouTube video, 01:53, posted August 19, 2012, accessed April 7, 2017: https://www.youtube.com/watch?v=19CHC7dFNoA. I retained the old English spelling. There are not spelling errors in the quote.

man. We believe God has called us to the impossible task of serving as his ambassador. We want to be obedient, so we go forth, reluctant but determined to tell people about him. We are determined because we know it's our privileged responsibility. We are reluctant because we believe we are set up for failure in this task. We project our own insecurities, doubts, and fears upon those we encounter. In return, we expect to be rejected. But what if we had a different approach? What if we believed that God, in his divine sovereignty and gracious compassion, was lovingly working on the lives of those we are called to reach? What if we believed God's Spirit was at work in the world, convicting and converting? Will we experience rejection? Certainly. Will we at times get into socially awkward situations? Sure. Anytime a counter-cultural message is presented, it will occasionally create problems. That should be expected because we have an enemy actively working against us. We understand that. What we often forget is that God is also working. God is preparing the hearts of people. Fertile soil has been prepared for the reception of the seed of God's Word, and as we scatter that seed, we should expect God to be working and preparing the hearts of listeners. We should expect God to be working to make our efforts effective. Maybe you've heard of the frustrated young Bible student who approached famed preacher Charles H. Spurgeon in the mid to late nineteenth century. He came to Spurgeon for advice because, despite all his preaching, he had not seen anyone come to faith in Jesus. Spurgeon retells this exchange,

> *You may have heard the story of one of our first students, who came to me, and said, "I have been preaching now for some months, and I do not think I have had a single conversion." I said to him, "And do you expect that the Lord is going to bless you and save souls every time you open your mouth?" "No, sir," he replied. "Well, then," I said, "that is why you do not get souls saved. If you had believed, the Lord would have given the blessing."*[43]

---

[43]C. H. Spurgeon, *The Soul-Winner; or, How to Lead Sinners to the Saviour* (New York: Fleming H. Revell, 1895), 52.

While we have no guarantee from the Lord that he will convert souls every time we preach the gospel, what I love about this quote is that it reminds us of the faith and confidence we should have in God's working power. We should believe God blesses his work. We should believe God will promote and expand his kingdom. We should expect God to be working in and through us as we go forth as his ambassadors. And we should not be surprised that the gospel itself contains power to save and reconcile others (Rom. 1:16). The power to change lives is not found in the vessel (we as God's ambassadors) but in the message we vessels carry. Consequently, we should realize that God is always faithful to himself and his word. God is working through us, powerfully reconciling to himself those who hear gospel by our verbal proclamations.

The third truth is: we are to be persistent in pursuing this purpose. How often do we go out as ambassadors and talk to someone about the gospel once and then give up? We don't follow up to re-engage the conversation. We merely check our responsibility off the chart and move on. How often do we invite our neighbors to church? Maybe once or twice? They say no, so we just give up on them. Now, as an aside, going to church doesn't make someone a Christian, and we should not use the church as our sole means of evangelism. That being said, we do live in a society where people test before they commit. People, at least in America, will often want to experience our churches and build relationship with Christians before deciding to give their life to Jesus. The role of church in reaching our neighbors is highly debated, but the point being made here is how quickly we tend to jettison our duties and opportunities as ambassadors. Are we persistent in pursuing our purpose? If someone offered us the chance for an all-expense paid trip to the World Series to see our favorite team play if we accomplished certain tasks, think about how hard we would work. The point is not that we work our way to heaven; the point is that, when it is something we are passionate about, we do not make excuses when obstacles arise; we persevere and find solutions. When we want something badly enough or believe in something deeply enough, we are persistent and endure. So why do we give up so quickly on our responsibility of living and proclaiming God's message as ambassadors? Let's be persistent and creative in pursuing our calling. Let's make a habit of talking to others about our lives while we prayerfully look for opportunities to share God's message for them. We can invite people over for dinner to get to know them better, build relationships with them, and seek to influence them with Christ. We can invite people to connect with us in our recreational time and see what doors the Lord might open. We can take people fishing or have them over to watch a mixed-martial-arts fight night. We can put together inexpensive holiday baskets with a small gift, an evangelistic tract, and personal letter inside, and deliver them to people who live in the neighborhood. When eating out, we can ask our server questions that open the door for spiritual conversations. One technique is to say, "Thanks for the food. It looks great. We are about to pray for our food and just wanted to know if there was anything we could pray for you?" This approach, if done casually and with honest interest, will regularly open up remarkable opportunities to talk with and pray for people in need. Regardless of the venues we seek to leverage for the sake of our ambassadorship, we are called to relentlessly pursue our purpose of making disciples. This calling to make disciples is a life calling God has placed upon each of his children. It's a calling that beckons us to live as ambassadors for him in our workplace, church, home, school, and even when on vacation. This calling isn't about getting a notch on the belt because we think we convinced someone to believe the way we do. This calling is about revealing amazing truths to others. It about revealing to others that God has provided a way to be reconciled to him, God invites them into that relationship, and once reconciled, God then wants to use them to reach others. As we go forth as ambassadors, let us pray God would open up opportunities, give us the wisdom to see those opportunities, and give us the courage to engage those opportunities.

When I was a kid who broke his arm playing football, I felt I had lost my purpose. The fact is that I hadn't lost my purpose. I just hadn't found it yet. My purpose was to be an ambassador for Jesus, and that's a purpose nothing in this world can take away. That purpose can be fulfilled in any vocation at any time in any place. We've been commissioned to promote the interest of a reconciling King. Despite our past failures or the failures of those around us, we must resist the urge to make excuses. We must not allow our calling to be defined by anything or anyone other than the One who calls us: God himself. God has given us a purpose. God has given us a role on his team. God wants us to be his ambassadors representing him to a world in desperate need of him. So, will we embrace this calling? Will we chance our arms?

Questions for Reflection

Have you ever wondered what God wants you to do? Have you ever questioned your purpose? What brought about these questions? How did you answer them?

After reading the chapter, how would you define the role of an ambassador? What does it mean to be ambassadors of Christ?

What makes sharing Christ with others difficult? What sometimes prevents us from speaking the Gospel to others?

Why does God call us to be persistent Gospel witnesses? Why can't we share once and be done?

Is there a specific person or group who God has called you to share his love with? How can others encourage you as you serve as Christ's ambassador?

CHAPTER 9
FAMILY: AGENTS OF GOD

Failure to Thrive

My (Matt's) grandpa liked to share winsome nuggets of wisdom like, "Every day, I get a little bit older." And the truth is, life changes as we age. Take, for example, the baby-boomer generation (people born between 1946 and 1964). The youngest boomers are entering middle-age, and the oldest boomers are in their seventies. Since the aging boomer generation is so large, geriatric medicine is becoming a field of focus in the medical community. One challenging condition in geriatric medicine is called *failure to thrive* (FTT), an illness the American Academy of Family Physicians defines as "a state of decline...caused by chronic concurrent diseases and functional impairments."[44] Simply put, people suffer from so many ailments that they simply refuse to care anymore. They give up.

One of the clearest signs of FTT is malnutrition. They refuse to care for their own bodies. Then malnutrition leads to severe depression, and a vicious downward spiral ensues. In order to save the life of someone with FTT, there is one critical step. Someone must notice. A family member must recognize that Grandma is losing weight or that she isn't caring for her own basic needs. If they identify the signs and get her to a medical professional, they have the option to pursue purposeful treatment. Together, family and physicians can try to stop the cycle.

---

[44]Russell G. Robertson and Marcos Montagnini, "Geriatric Failure to Thrive," *American Family Physician* 70.2 (2004): 343–350.

In my years as a Christian, I've seen people of all ages suffering with a spiritual form of FTT. They become spiritually lethargic. Spiritual "nutrition" is no longer a concern. They avoid God and then feel as if he has abandoned them. Faith is no longer joyful but a grind. Every form of spiritual health and vitality disappears because they refuse to care anymore. They give up.

When people suffer from physical FTT, the obvious first step is to get them to the doctor. But what about those who struggle in the Christian life? Where is the spiritual doctor who can assess our pain? Who will prescribe a course of treatment? Who will even notice our struggles at all? The answer is actually quite simple. The solution is the church.

The Warning Passages

Much like those suffering from FTT, members of the audience of Hebrews were spiritually malnourished in spite of their advancing years of Christian commitment. In Hebrews 5:12, the author laments, "In fact, though by this time you ought to be teachers, you need someone to teach you the elementary truths of God's word all over again. You need milk, not solid food!" The phrase "by this time" shows that the church was not a fledgling congregation. They had some history. In fact, Hebrews 2:3–4 suggests that some of the original disciples of Jesus shared the Gospel story and helped form the Hebrews congregation. Yet, in spite of the church's age, the congregation hadn't grown in the only way that matters—spiritually. They were older but not wiser. In fact, they needed a refresher course on the basics of faith. The author needed to put away the steak and potatoes and return to infant formula.

As a result of the audience's need, the author penned five warning passages, often delineated as follows: Hebrews 2:1–4; 3:7— 4:13; 6:4–8; 10:26–39; and 12:1–29. Scholars and theologians have spilled a lot of ink discussing the impact of the warnings on the doctrine of salvation. These are important debates with real-life implications. But we who major in the minor details of theology sometimes miss the forest for the trees. For example, many have written page after page on the theology of the warnings without asking a critical question. What did the author of Hebrews hope to accomplish when he penned the warning passages? Why did the author issue warnings at all? And what was his desired outcome for church members who read (or listened to) Hebrews week after week?

I think the answer to these questions is a lot more practical than the big theological discussions would suggest. Simply put, the author warns *the church* to watch out for struggling members. Some in the community exhibit signs of failure to thrive; therefore, the church must nurse them back to spiritual health.

For the author of Hebrews, spiritual healing was not an individualistic endeavor in which each believer sits alone in a room and reflects on his or her Christian commitment. There are no Lone Ranger Christians. Instead, one reason God designed the church was to protect each individual member. The church is a family meant to notice those with spiritual FTT and pursue treatment for their spiritual decline. The Hebrews warning passages call the whole congregation to actively exhort struggling church members to remain faithful.

Moving forward, then, let's look at the warning passages and see the essential role of the family of God. We'll start with the warning that stands at the center of the book, found in Hebrews 6:4–8.

A Plea for Teachers

The zenith of the third warning appears in Hebrews 6:4–8, but the introduction begins in 5:11–14. There, the author shifts from *celebrating* the priestly ministry of Jesus to *condemning* the audience's failure to thrive. We already mentioned Hebrews 5:12, where the author chastises those who ought to be teachers after so much time. The implication is that the congregation *should* be equipped to teach, but it has failed to mature. Implicit in the author's critique is the conviction that each individual is obligated to grow into personal maturity so that he or she might benefit the corporate body. In other words, spiritual growth isn't merely for my own benefit. Like a tea pitcher, the goal is to be filled in order to pour out.

We also see that the teaching ministry of the church is vital. It isn't enough to find a church with rockin' worship and a state-of-the-art playground. Youth summer trips, men's ministry campouts, and fellowship dinners are all great. But if the church doesn't disciple its members, it is missing the mark. So, if you're starting at square one looking for a church to join, find a congregation that emphasizes the teaching of God's Word. Ask leaders how the church disciples its members, how they teach and train those of all ages. And land in a church family that provides spiritual milk *and* steak.

Back in Hebrews, we see the author model his conviction beginning in 6:1. He proposes to finally lead his audience beyond the basics of faith. As the parent of a three-year-old, I feel for the author. Nothing is more tiring than repeating the same instruction time and again. In our house, we often talk about "first-time obedience." Listen to me. Think about it. And do what needs to be done. The author of Hebrews wanted the same from his congregation. They need first-time understanding of the basics of faith so that they can pass along what they learn. "It's the last time I'm going to say this," we can almost hear him say, "so pay attention this time!"

In case the audience isn't yet motivated to obey, the author describes in 6:4–5 an alarming scenario that should motivate community members to mature—namely, the possibility that some within the community may drift away. The author portrays a hypothetical scenario in which someone sees God do incredible things. God enlightens the mind, shows the power of the Holy Spirit, and enables miraculous acts (which he calls "the powers of the age to come"). Scot McKnight has rightly labeled the experiences of verses 4–5 as signs of "phenomenological faith."[45] In other words, these outward phenomena, which likely occur during church

---

[45] Scot McKnight, "The Warning Passages of Hebrews: A Formal Analysis and Theological Conclusions," *Trinity Journal* 13 (1992): 21–59.

gatherings, suggest to the congregation that an individual seems to trust in Jesus.

I like to think of "phenomenological faith" like watching live TV. When you watch the Super Bowl, you don't think about the director in a room full of screens calling out which camera angle the audience should see. You never consider all of the sound engineers on the sidelines, the people feeding information to the commentators, or the dozens of camera operators. All you see is what shows up on your screen. The same is true spiritually. As humans, all we see is what is right in front of us. On the other hand, 1 Samuel 16:7 says, "The LORD does not look at the things people look at. People look at the outward appearance, but the LORD looks at the heart." So, God is like the Super Bowl director, who knows what is happening all over the stadium at any given time. But we're only seeing what's on TV.

When we look back at Hebrews 6:4–5, then, the author describes a scenario in which someone is doing well in his or her Christian life. The church can see evidence that he trusts in Jesus. But then he hits a bump in the road. Verse 6 describes the "bump" as "falling away." This vague phrase likely points to a *public* incident within the church. In other words, the congregation is able to recognize a member who is failing to thrive. The author then uses harsh language to describe the consequences of unchecked spiritual FTT. The worst is that the untreated member could bring shame upon the name of Jesus.

Why did the author write this warning? Is it a scare tactic, meant to make us all doubt God's work in our lives? I don't think so. In fact, I don't think the author's primary goal is personal introspection. Instead, the possibility that a fellow church member could shame Jesus is meant to shock the church! The implication is that the Christian family must not let individual sin slide, must not ignore the "slow fade," because it has a devastating result. We cannot become so focused on ourselves that we ignore the struggles of others. The church family must watch for signs of failure to thrive.

The author follows his warning with a brief parable about good and bad soil (6:7–8). His broader purpose, though, is shown in his description of the good soil. It receives a blessing from God because it is *beneficial to others*. In other words, my Christian walk isn't just for me. It should nourish my fellow believers as well. In contrast, the thorny harvest of verse 8 is worthless because it benefits no one— God or human. Again, there is no place for self-centered, individualistic Christian practice. The church is a critical source of nourishment for the individual Christian. Those who avoid the family of God not only neglect the protection of the community but also prevent the congregation from benefiting from their own Christian fruit. Lone Ranger Christianity is a lose-lose.

With a sigh of relief, we move in 6:9–12 to a word of praise from the author. He was confident that his audience would respond rightly to his warnings, but not for the reasons you might think. His confidence was not in their mission statement, financial growth, or any of the factors we often use to measure church health today. Actually, the sign of success is that they serve one another. Their teaching ministry may not be up to par yet, but they have consistently served each other, which is really an act of love toward God.

In case you missed it, let me restate this important truth. Caring for the family of God is an act of worship. We tend to limit "worship" to singing songs to God on Sunday mornings. Maybe we would add reading the Bible and praying as "worship," but few include ministry to the church body as worship. Yet the author of Hebrews suggests that we show our love for God by loving his children. The result, then, is that we can't worship God in every possible way unless we care for fellow believers.

Throughout the central warning, we've seen Hebrews highlight the importance of the church family. Christian community should be a beacon of Biblical teaching, feeding those in all spiritual stages. The church also watches for struggling members in order to treat their failure to thrive. When individual believers come together as the family of God, we find nourishment from the fruit of one another's lives. Finally, the church provides an opportunity to worship by serving God's children—our brothers and sisters.

The Daily Task

Hebrews 6 is not the only difficult passage in the author's lengthy sermon. In fact, earlier in the letter, he demanded that the whole community watch one another's lives daily. His instructions began in Hebrews 3:12 with the call to prevent any one of them from having an evil, unbelieving heart. You *are* your brother's keeper. It's not enough to focus on your own Christian walk; you have to protect others as well.

We began the chapter with some contemporary problems among the baby boomer generation. But other generations have their issues, too. I'm a millennial. I also teach college students who are on the boundary of the millennial generation. We millennials are often described as inherently relational, craving human connection above all else. But what kind of "connection" do we want? I would argue that, while we want relationships, many are content with shallow ones. We want thousands of Facebook friends so they can see the amazing vegan dish we made for dinner. But we don't want anyone close enough to see our flaws. And if people try to point out my destructive tendencies, I'll unfriend them all! I mean, who are they to judge me?

My fear is that this shallow view of "friendship" can spill over into the church. We view our Christian family as people who can encourage us but who should never confront us. If they do, they're judgmental. They're hypocrites. Yet, in 1 Corinthians 5:12, Paul asked two questions to kindly instruct the church to avoid passing judgment on non-believers while simultaneously watching out for sin within the church. In fact, the whole chapter addresses sin within the church. Paul criticized the congregation for ignoring blatant immorality among its members. According to Paul, true love will confront sin so that the sinner may be rescued at the end (see verse 5). Like the doctor who ignores cancer in his patient, the church that ignores the individual sin does no one any favors.

The author of Hebrews agreed with Paul, and he offers a solution in Hebrews 3:13. He claims that a Sunday service is not enough. Individuals might harden their hearts any day of the week, so we must exhort one another every day called "today." In case you're not catching on, he means every single day. The daily task of the Christian family is to exhort one another. But what does exhortation look like? Well, in Hebrews 13:22, he called his letter a "word of exhortation." So, Hebrews itself is the model of Christian exhortation.

Within Hebrews, we see words of encouragement, warnings, Scripture quotations, discussions about Jesus, instructions, and much more. That means we are to exhort one another every day by encouraging one another. When you see God working in your Christian sister's life, tell her. Let her know how God is using her to enable greater faithfulness and worship in your own life. If you see a sophomore in high school disconnecting from the youth ministry because he got his license and wants to "be free," call him out. Warn him about the difficulty of trying to love Jesus by himself. When you see a brother in Christ struggling with insecurity because he lost his job, text him Bible verses about God's unconditional love and faithfulness. For the little girl who doesn't know how to pray, instruct her. No matter what day of the week it is and no matter what each person needs, believers are called to exhort one another constantly.

Before we move on, I want to clarify something. The author of Hebrews is writing to the whole congregation, not just its leaders. Consequently, the call to "exhort one another daily" is for all, not just pastors or elders. Church leaders are not the only people who can address sin. Instead, God designed us all to correct one another. Unfortunately, because many of us are afraid to confront habitual sin in those closest to us, it puts a greater burden on church leadership. The result is that leaders minister with grief and not joy (see Hebrews 13:17). But even more problematic is that struggling Christians don't hear from their closest friends—the very people who have the best chance of getting through to them. So, as the family of God, we need to move beyond shallow relationships, at least with our closest believing friends. We desperately need each

Christian to engage in a daily ministry of exhortation, so that the body of Christ can be healthy.

The Provocative Church

As if the author of Hebrews hadn't made his point yet, he returns to the same theme in Hebrews 10:19–25. He first summarizes what he said in Hebrews 7–10, recounting the unrestrained access to God that believers experience because of the sacrifice of Jesus. For Hebrews, access to God's throne is the heart of the Gospel. In fact, one of my favorite verses in the Bible is Hebrews 4:16: "Let us then approach God's throne of grace with confidence, so that we may receive mercy and find grace to help us in our time of need." Praise God that we can draw near to him because of the death of Jesus!

In light of our access to God's presence, the author issues three instructions in Hebrews 10:22–24. The church should draw near to God, hold to their hope, and consider how to provoke what is good in one another. First, if we *can* know God, we *should*. Draw near to God! Second, don't give up. Maintain the hope you've held since the beginning. Third, give yourself to your church. This final instruction deserves closer consideration.

The author expected church members to consider how to help one another, looking for opportunities to promote love and good deeds. Actually, the verb the author used is "to provoke." As in English, the word provoke often has a negative connotation in Greek. For example, fathers should not provoke their children to anger. But provocation can also be positive.

My wife and I competed in an event called a "Tough Mudder." Essentially, it is a half-marathon mixed with a sadistic obstacle course. I say sadistic because one of the "obstacles" was a giant tank full of ice water. You slide down a ramp, completely submerge yourself in the arctic bath, and then have to will your muscles into obedience to swim out. The final obstacle, though, is even worse — or at least even scarier. You run through mud and leap over hay bales. That part wouldn't be so bad except that hundreds of live wires hang from a trellis overhead. Honestly, it's a lot more fun to watch

135

than to do. I admit I was amused to see big burly men hit an electric wire and drop face first into the mud. But the amusement dies when you're next in line.

So, when our team got to this final obstacle, several of us froze, not wanting to face "electroshock therapy." But we knew the finish line was just on the other side. There was nowhere to go but through it. Cleverly, the creators of the event put an obnoxious guy with a microphone at the entrance to the final obstacle. It was apparently his job to provoke us into action. Without him, I'm not sure many would run the gauntlet to cross the finish line. He was annoying, constantly counting down, as if that would force me to run. But honestly, I'm not sure I would have finished if he hadn't provoked me to go.

In 10:24, the author of Hebrews calls the church to be that annoying guy with the microphone. The Christian family cannot force people to do what is right, but we can irritate or excite one another to action. We can call one another to love and good deeds. We can challenge, encourage, and exhort. But something else must happen first. To speak into one another's lives, we have to be around each other.

Hebrews 10:25 instructs the church not to forsake gathering together. Simply put, scattered church members can neither exhort one another nor stimulate love and good deeds. Apparently, some in the Hebrews community had habitually forsaken community gatherings. They are skipping church. Why they're missing is a mystery, but the result is clear. They were suffering, and so was the church. In his commentary, Gary Cockerill accurately sums up the consequence, noting, "Those who 'abandon' other believers leave them in the lurch and thus deprive their brothers and sisters of needed support."[46] Christians have a responsibility to *attend* church gatherings. But the reason is not that church attendance is required

---

[46] Cockerill, *The Epistle to the Hebrews*, NICNT (Grand Rapids: Eerdmans, 2012), 479.

in order to be saved or to earn a gold star in heaven. No, we gather in order to provoke one another to follow Christ. We stand at the entrance of the obstacle challenging each another to keep going, to cross the finish line ("as you see the Day approaching").

I often ask people why they come to worship services. One common answer I hear is "I want to feel God's presence." There's nothing wrong—and actually everything right—with wanting to experience God. But church gatherings are not merely conduits of spiritual introspection and individual contemplation. Gatherings are also designed to glorify God by means of mutual provocation. Believers are not to forsake church gatherings but are to come together and "encourage one another." This same idea is presented in 3:13. Like a good preacher, the author is driving his point home through repetition: get together and encourage one another.

In the harsh warning that follows (10:26–31), the author again attempts to shock the church into action. If they don't exhort those who are failing to thrive—failing even to come to church—the results could be dire. Then in 10:32–34, the author recalls the church's past concern for those struggling to complete an obstacle. In the past, some members of the Hebrews community endured suffering. They were attacked publicly. Some even had their homes taken away. Others were imprisoned. But the church stuck together. Those who personally suffered persecution did not turn inward and drift from the community. No, they identified with others who also suffered. The community even showed sympathy to those who were imprisoned. The church watched after those most at risk of failure to thrive, and they had great success.

Many of us have a similar story. When we lost my father-in-law to cancer four years ago, our church stepped up. People brought us food, gift cards, even paper products. We received sympathy cards, hopeful notes, thoughtful texts, and verbal words of encouragement regularly. At his funeral, we sang songs of worship together as we mourned our incredible loss. And the truth is, I don't know I could have survived without my Christian family. And that's coming from a pastor who was working on his PhD in Biblical Studies. I knew most of the right answers to my questions, but I needed my brothers and sisters to watch out for me and exhort me to endure. And that need continues.

Broken Legs and Bitter Roots

We're almost done, but there's one more warning passage. The warning spans all of Hebrews 12, but we'll focus on verses 1–17. The final warning passage follows the presentation of faithful witnesses in chapter 11—people who suffered but remained faithful to God. Hebrews 11 details their "survival stories." These survivors surround the church today (12:1), encouraging and exhorting us with their life stories. In 12:1–3, the author challenges believers to imitate the cloud of faithful witnesses who endured hardship, looking principally to the example of Jesus. Our Savior faced suffering with joy, and now he reigns in heaven at the right hand of God.

Next, Hebrews 12:4–13 assures the audience that God allows suffering in order to train and correct his children. God is a better parent than I am. He knows when to allow struggle and when to offer help in order to shape us into his image. One of those shaping forces is the care of our brothers and sisters who protect us from injury.

Like my reference to FTT throughout this chapter, the author used a medical metaphor in verse 12–13. He pictured those who drift from God as crippled feet, knees, or legs that become dislocated because of improper or excessive use. One may suppose that the spiritually disabled are the same members who risk hardening their hearts and falling away according to the previous warning passages. Their failure to thrive has caused bodily damage that may become permanent if the church shirks its role. In order to avoid lasting damage, the whole church must prevent the lame from becoming dislocated and must make straight paths with their feet. We must reach out. We must bear their burdens. We must pick up their slack. By doing so, we create "straight paths" and prevent needless, painful wandering. Prayerfully, such measures will stimulate healing in those failing to thrive.

Leaving the metaphor behind, the author calls his audience in 12:15 to watch for a "bitter root" who might harm and defile the community. The image of a bitter root comes from Deuteronomy 29:18. There, Moses warns about a person who thinks he or she can disobey covenant obligations while enjoying the favor of God. Think of people who believe that going to church cancels out their abusive behavior or sexual sin. Or what about that family at church that spreads gossip or complains about every decision? They call their gossip "prayer" and their complaints "constructive criticism," but they're really just bitter roots.

The unfortunate truth is that the Christian family includes bitter roots. We all struggle with sin, but some continually hurt those around them with their sin. Maybe you've encountered a church member like that. She hurt you. He betrayed you. And now you don't know if you can trust the church again. My appeal to you is that you don't quit. Give the family of God another chance. Even better, forgive as you have been forgiven. I don't claim forgiveness is easy. Yet, when the disciples ask Jesus how often to forgive their brothers and sisters, he tells them seventy times seven. It's a symbolic way to say, "Don't stop forgiving!"

At the same time, Hebrews 12:15 informs the congregation to watch out so that *no one* will live such a life. The author may have been beating a dead horse here, but the challenge remains the same. The church must watch over all. Every individual needs the care of the community. And every community is at risk when individuals become "bitter roots." So, in your role as a church member, keep your eyes open and help those who hurt themselves or others. Exhort them daily.

Living It Out

Spiritual failure to thrive is a real concern. Even those who follow Jesus suffer seasons of weakness and frailty. All of us are only one bad decision away from ruining our testimony. So, who will protect us? Who will watch for signs of FTT in our lives? Praise God, he has met our need by providing the church. Our Christian brothers and sisters are the agents of God, watching and protecting us from decline. We don't expect anguished church members to treat their own wounds. The church must notice FTT and bring struggling members to the Great Physician. Only in his arms is healing found.

According to Hebrews, then, there is no room for rugged individualism in the Christian walk. God did not design you to be a Lone Ranger Christian. As church members, we need one another. We need to grow in maturity so that we can teach others. Our lives should produce spiritual fruit that benefits the body. We must exhort one another daily and serve as an act of worship. When it gathers, the Christian family should provoke love and good deeds. Those who suffer in circumstances that could easily draw them away must benefit from the church's care, sympathy, and support. And we must realize the devastating results of ignoring sin within the body.

What about you? Have you connected to a Christian family? Do you have the support of a community of faithful saints? I challenge you to attend worship services, Sunday School classes, and discipleship events. I also encourage you to pursue deep Christian relationships. Don't settle for shallow "Facebook Friend" relationships in the church. You need to know people and be known. Find people who will exhort you and receive your exhortations. And by the grace of God, the church's efforts will help us all to persevere in hope until we join the great cloud of witnesses.

Questions for Reflection:

Have you seen examples of spiritual failure to thrive? What did it look like? What were the symptoms?

What makes participating in the church most difficult?

Describe a time when you have been encouraged, corrected, or helped by another believer? What caused the church to reach out? How did it impact you?

Are there believers in your life you can exhort? What are some concrete, practical ways you can provoke them to love and good deeds?

Is there a wounded individual who needs your help or the church's help? How can you reach out this week?

CHAPTER 10
FUTURE: SECURED BY GOD

Wedding Bells Shattered

In the mid 1980s, Walker Books approached Martin Handford and asked him to illustrate a book featuring large crowds.[47] Within those crowds, it was suggested that he create some type of focal point. The idea was to create something within the picture that people would look for rather than just glancing at the picture as a whole. Handford went to work and created "Wally," a ditsy world traveler who was constantly lost and dressed in red and white stripes. The work was an immediate success. While published in the UK as "Wally", this same series was published in the US as "Where's Waldo?" He became immensely popular simply by providing a pictorial focal point. Audiences everywhere have been entertained ever since by trying to find Waldo in various types of pictures, and as elusive as Waldo was, he was always there. The focal point made all the difference.

---

[47]Paul Bignell, "Where's the brains behind Wally?" The Independent, November 12, 2011, accessed April 14, 2017, http://www.independent.co.uk/arts-entertainment/books/news/wheres-the-brains-behind-wally-6261459.html, Phil Edwards, "Who's Waldo? The early history of Martin Handford's Waldo," Trivia Happy, October 22, 2014, accessed April 14, 2017, https://triviahappy.com/articles/whos-waldo-the-early-history-of-martin-handfords-waldo; Cyndi Stivers, "Where's Waldo?" EW.com, December 14, 1990, accessed April 14, 2017, http://ew.com/article/1990/12/14/wheres-waldo/; Emily Upton, "The Origin of 'Where's Waldo,'" Today I Found Out, August 28, 2013, accessed April 14, 2017, http://www.todayifoundout.com/index.php/2013/08/the-history-of-wheres-waldo/.

In a similar way, God has provided a focal point in life to bring hope, yet finding hope in the midst of the picture of life is often frustrating. Hope seems hidden, elusive, and sometimes absolutely absent from the picture life is painting. Have you been there? Have you ever been in a situation where life seemed to end? From the outside perspective, your current crisis might seem petty or insignificant, but for you who are going through it, the crisis feels dark, debilitating, and hopeless. We've all been there. I (Adam) was eleven years old, and my father was asked to officiate a wedding. There was a catch, however. The couple getting married did not have anyone to play an instrument, so a recording of the wedding march "Here Comes the Bride" was to be played over the sound system. Since my father was officiating, he involuntarily committed me. Great! He had the eleven-year-old poster child for ADHD in charge of this special moment. Honestly, I don't think it would have been too bad—except I was in a room with no visual of the ceremony. I respectfully protested to my father on these terms, but he insisted that it would be no problem. He explained, "Look, there's a long pause at the end of the song, and that's when you will press stop." Okay. "I can do this," I told myself. My father reassured me and left the room. It was time. I pressed play. I heard a pause. I pressed stop. Case closed. I nailed it. At least, I had nailed it, until fifteen seconds later when my father ran into the room to tell me I had pressed stop too soon with the bride only two-thirds of the way down the aisle. Everyone was watching. I had just ruined a woman's most important day. I was so embarrassed that I hid in that back room. After the ceremony when the people had left for the reception, my dad came for me. I was mortified. I felt as if the world had ended. Hope had vanished like smoke on a windy day. Have you been there? Maybe:

- ❖ your spouse of fifty years passed away.

- ❖ you get a call that your child is a drug addict and locked up.

- ❖ the person you thought loved you broke up with you and took someone else to the prom.

❖ your colicky baby has been up for two nights screaming, and you just can't handle it.

❖ you were laid off, and your pension dissolved.

❖ you're being sued by someone you used to trust.

It is in these crowded life pictures that we need hope the most. So, what is our focal point for hope, and what difference does it make? Let's look together into Paul's encouragement to Titus for that answer (Titus 2:11–14).

Everyone Struggles

The Apostle Paul had left Titus behind in Crete to lead the efforts in creating order and structure for the young church there (Titus 1:5). This church was under attack. False teachers in the church were promoting corrupt theology and confusing those in attendance. Titus' first order of business was to establish elders to shepherd, teach, and lead the church. Additionally, he was to silence these false teachers (1:5–16). In contrast to these false teachers, Titus was implored throughout the process to ensure sound doctrine was taught to each segment of the church populous whether they were older, younger, free, or slave (2:1–10). One interesting component of this section is that Titus was charged to address various groups in the church by confronting areas that could bring frustration and potential hopelessness: areas these false teachers had exploited. For example, he was to teach older men to control their tempers and not allow the frustrations of this world to dictate their behavior (2:2). He was to instruct older women to watch how they spoke about others and to control their alcohol intake (2:3). (With low life expectancies, high infant mortality rates, high rates of widowhood, limited clean water, and many other life-troubles, there were plenty of depressing issues existed to contribute to overindulging in wine.) Paul directed Titus to teach younger women to love their families and be faithful in their daily responsibilities. Titus was also instructed to teach younger men to be self-controlled and to teach slaves to be obedient and respectful to their masters (2:4–10). Let's be clear. This list of needed instruction existed because these were real struggles for these people. Submitting in these areas would be hard. Paul knew the people would need a focal point to guide them through the varied crowded emotions that would press in on them throughout their day. Paul also knew from personal experience that God had provided such a focal point to bring hope for such times, and he presented it in verses eleven through fourteen of chapter two. Let's carefully look at those together.

Grace Appears

God's grace suddenly erupted through "our moral darkness, like a rising sun" offering salvation.[48] What a glorious thought that God's grace has shined upon us. The Apostle Paul describes grace as something that has been suddenly and plainly revealed to us. He then explains how this beautiful grace serves as the basis and focal point for his command to live godly in the midst of this broken world. He writes, "For the grace of God has appeared that offers salvation to all people" (2:11). A question immediately emerges that deserves attention before continuing. When did this grace of God appear to us? Paul wasn't merely writing about a moment of experience; he was writing about a moment of revelation. God revealed the essence of grace: a grace that offered salvation. When did this happen? God's grace was revealed to us in the birth, life, death, and resurrection of Jesus.[49] Jesus' life was the tangible manifestation of God's saving grace for all people regardless of social status, ethnicity, or gender.[50] God's manifestation of universal

---

[48]This verb is where we get our word "epiphany...and conveys the image of grace suddenly breaking in on our moral darkness, like the rising sun" (D. Edmond Hiebert, "Titus" in *The Expositor's Bible Commentary* (Grand Rapids: Zondervan, 1981), 439.

[49]Thomas D. Lea and Hayne P. Griffin, *1, 2 Timothy, Titus*, vol. 34, NAC (Nashville: B&H, 1992), 310.

[50]While this section follows immediately after addressing slaves, Paul makes it clear here that this hope is not reserved only for them but for all types or classes of people. God's salvation isn't reserved only for a selected

grace was for the world to see, to know, and to accept. What an amazing thought. Jesus is the proof of God's loving grace, yet, despite this revelation of grace, it is still easy for doubts to come. The varied circumstances of life can quickly overwhelm us and cause us to question many things concerning God. Is God real? Does God really love me? How can God be good in light of these circumstances I'm experiencing? Some skeptics may even contend that if God would just prove himself to them, then they would trust him. Scott Stapp falls into this category. In 2000, Stapp was the lead singer of Creed, the most popular hard-rock band in the America. He did an interview with *Spin* magazine talking about his life, faith, and doubts.

> *"I tell you, [my son] is a spitting image of me. You love to see yourself in your children, but I don't want him to have the same personality as me...I just don't want him to have the same demons that I have. I don't want him always thinking about the grand scheme of things—life and death and heaven and hell and good and bad. That's the cross I bear daily..."*

> *"My whole life was church,"* Stapp says. *He had Bible study on Friday evenings and attended services every Wednesday night, twice on Sunday. He was forced to wear a necktie to high school. His weekend curfew was 10 P.M. "I would sit in my room and wish I could go to parties after the football game,"* Stapp remembers. *"I wished I could go to the prom. I felt weird: I felt different."*

> *In church, when the spirit of God passed over them, people would suddenly start speaking in tongues, falling on the floor in ecstasy. It never happened to Stapp, and he couldn't understand why God kept passing him over. "I thought something was wrong with me, so I lived with a*

---

group or class, but is extended to all. See Newport J. D. White, "Titus" in *The Expositor's Greek Testament* (Grand Rapids: Eerdmans, 1976), 194.

lot of guilt," he recalls. "I constantly found myself asking God to prove himself to me...I'd lie in bed and say, 'God, if you're real, just make my light go off so I won't doubt it. I promise I'll be the best Christian in the world.'"[51]

My heart hurts for those like Stapp because I've been there. "If God would only [fill in the blank], I'd be the best Christian in the world," we think. However, would the lights flickering on and off, as in Stapp's request, really provide a sufficient sign of the existence of God to such an extent that we would never doubt again? How would we know it wasn't a power surge? Is such a sign really sufficient to sustain our faith in the wake of the death of our child, the foreclosure of our home, the bad medical diagnosis, or the abandonment of our significant other? Such feelings of doubt about God are understandable, and we need a sign, a proof of God's existence and love that will concretely be able to visibly stand despite all the crashing waves of this turbulent life. We need a sign that can always be found in the chaotic picture of life: a sign upon which we can focus our faith. The truth is that God has invaded human history and proven not only his existence but also that his love for us is beyond question. Jesus is that proof. Jesus himself explains that the ultimate proof he really was the Son of God was his death, bodily resurrection, and the empty tomb (Matt. 12:38–42). If Jesus really rose from the dead, what further proof do we need? If Jesus really died for our sins and rose from the dead, what other proof could possibly satisfy our doubts? Through Jesus, God proved the extent of his unfailing love. He now offers to rescue us from sin by extending his incomprehensible grade to us. God's real presence and grace was manifested through the life, death, and resurrection of Jesus Christ, and if we will listen to this grace, it teaches us to live differently.

---

[51]Gavin Edwards, "Sea of Fire," *Spin* (September 2000), 111.

Grace the Teacher

Let's see how Paul describes the transforming grace revealed through the person and work of Jesus.

> It [grace] teaches us to say "No" to ungodliness and worldly passions, and to live self-controlled, upright and godly lives in this present age, while we wait for the blessed hope—the appearing of the glory of our great God and Savior, Jesus Christ, who gave himself for us to redeem us from all wickedness and to purify for himself a people that are his very own, eager to do what is good.

Titus 2:12–14.

God's grace as manifested through Jesus trains us to live differently. This revealed grace teaches us to stop doing some things and start doing other things. Through the power of God's revealed grace, we are called to deny ungodly and worldly passions that are contrary to the will of God. In contrast, we are to submit ourselves to him and "live self-controlled, upright, and godly lives in this present age." Paul's use of the phrase "this present age presupposes another, future age for which the Christian believer hopes with assurance and perseverance."[52] In other words, Paul challenged us to live now in anticipation of something better in the future.

Because of this grace, we are not just called to live holy lives in the future; we are called to live holy lives now, "while we wait for the blessed hope." The word "hope" as used in this text is not how we tend to use "hope" in our culture. Normally, when we think of hope, we think of a "wish." For example, whenever we go to the county fair, we walk around eating hot dogs and having fun. We see these fun rides everywhere, walk up, and get in line. As we get closer to the front of the line, we hear the creaking of the metal, see the flaking of the paint, and see the rust of the bolts. We wonder when the last time this portable machine was inspected. Then, before we know it, it is our turn to get on the ride, and we think,

---

[52]Lea & Griffin, *1, 2, Timothy, Titus*, 311.

"Oh, I *hope* this doesn't break!" Here's another example. A teenage girl is walking through the mall, and she sees a cute guy. They begin to talk, and in the back of her mind, she thinks, "I *hope* he likes me." That's how we use the word "hope," but such usage is far from what the biblical writers had in mind. "Hope" is used in the Bible as a "confident expectation" (Gal. 5:5; Col. 1:5). It is an internal certainty that gives one confidence despite circumstances. This understanding is why Hebrews 11:1 explained that "faith is confidence in what we hope for and assurance about what we do not see." And what is this blessed hope for which we confidently anticipate? It is "the appearing of the glory of our great God and Savior, Jesus Christ" (Titus 2:13b). Our blessed hope is the appearing, the return of, "our great God and Savior," specifically Jesus the Christ. Don't miss the description Paul gave here. Jesus is our "God" and "Savior."[53] This God-man Jesus, who came to Earth and lived and died as our atoning sacrifice, "gave himself for us to redeem us from all wickedness and to purify for himself a people that are his very own, eager to do what is good" (Titus 2:14).

Jesus is coming back again. He promised to return for his followers multiple times (Matt. 24:30; John 14:1–3). Jesus will burst once again onto the scene in the future. We don't know when, but we know he's coming. That's our hope. It is such hope that grounds

---

[53]Such a confession is similar to that of the Apostle Thomas when he was saw Jesus for the first time after the resurrection and spoke to him saying, "My Lord and my God" (John 20:28)! A debate does exist as to whether "our great God and Savior" refers to two distinct beings or one, i.e. the person of Jesus. We could think about it this way. Is it "Our great God and Savior" or "Our great God" and then "our great Savior Jesus?" The structure of the text is that God and Savior describe Jesus Christ; thus, reading "our great God and Savior Jesus." That seems to be the most natural reading of the text. See also, Lea & Griffin, *1, 2, Timothy, Titus*, 312–14; A. T. Robertson, *A Grammar of the Greek New Testament in the Light of Historical Research* (Nashville: Broadman, 1934), 786–87; Daniel B. Wallace, *Greek Grammar beyond the Basics: An Exegetical Syntax of the New Testament* (Grand Rapids: Zondervan, 1996), 276. For an alternate opinion see White, "Titus," 195.

us through the storms of life. It is such hope that enables us not to lose heart and not to lose faith. Such a focus allows us to remember that despite the difficulty of living in this world, we have a Lord and Savior who is coming back again to bring to completion our redemption. In light of the return of Jesus, not only do we have hope; we also have motivation for living right in this present age in anticipation of the next.

Staying Focused

Some people get so caught up in prophecy (end times) charts that they miss the main purpose of God providing prophetic information in the Bible. We may not have thought about Titus 2:11–14 in that regard before, but look at it. These verses are about the return of Jesus. So let us pause here and look at two specific ways this passage should influence us as we faithful await Jesus' return.

First, we see that we are to live confidently! We should. We should have a confident expectation of Jesus' return to establish a new kingdom that impacts our attitude on earth. Back in 2014, in Springfield, Missouri, two of my daughters were hanging out with my wife Adrienne and me. Meagan was ten at the time, and Marigrace was nine. While we were out running errands, we had to go to the courthouse to get a new driver's license and a new tag for our car. We got to the Department of Motor Vehicles (DMV) in downtown Springfield, and while standing in line, my wife and I read a sign that stated we needed our birth certificates, social security cards, and proof of residence. "You've got to be kidding me," we exclaimed. "Here we've drug these kiddos all over the city, and now we have to go back home and get these documents just to come back up here to stand in line all over again." On the way back home to get the paperwork, Marigrace started complaining. "This is boring." "I want to stay home." Now, what she didn't know was that we had planned a special afternoon for them. As soon as we were done with the paperwork, we were going to take them to a place called "Incredible Pizza." (If you aren't familiar with this business, just know that any company with the name "incredible" and "pizza" in the title is amazing!) But here we were wasting another hour on paperwork while one of our children began to complain. Great. After a few more whiny comments from her, I was done. I said, "Fine. When we get home, you can stay while the rest of us go out for the day." My wife piped in, "But we were going to—" "That doesn't matter," I interrupted, "She'll just have to miss." At this point, Marigrace picked up on the fact that something better was coming. Her attitude completely changed. We got everything we thought we needed and once again stood in line only to find out that our car had to first have an inspection, which we didn't previously know about. So, we wasted all that time for nothing. But guess what? Marigrace didn't complain—not even a little. Why? She didn't complain because she knew that something better was waiting. She didn't know exactly what it was, but she knew it would be worth the wait. She was right. After the second attempt at the DMV, we were done. We threw the paperwork in the car and headed to Incredible Pizza, where we ate and played for the next four and a half hours. Her confidence that something better was coming changed her attitude and perspective.

What about you? Does the thought of Jesus coming again for his children motivate a confident hope within you? Thanks to Jesus' return:

- ❖ you don't have to be envious of other people's homes. Your home is temporary, and so is theirs. They are actually renting and don't know it. They will not keep their home forever, and neither will you. Jesus is coming back again to bring you to the glorious eternal home he is preparing for you.

- ❖ that dead-end job doesn't define you. Jesus wants you to serve him in anticipation of his return, even when others don't appreciate your work.

- ❖ that dented fender on your new vehicle from the hit and run in the parking lot is okay. Not only will your car be turned to scrap metal one day, but everything in this world decays over time. The possessions of this world are not your eternal hope.

❖ the death of a loved one or miscarriage doesn't have to break you. Jesus is coming to take you to a place where death will be no more.

❖ the traffic jam that's making you late for that appointment doesn't have to ruin your world. It's okay. Life will go on. Something more is waiting.

❖ what your classmates say about you in school isn't really important since Jesus is someday returning for you. Where he will take you is glorious, and never again will anyone ever say anything hurtful towards you.

This perspective doesn't mean that you will be emotionless. The truth of Jesus' return doesn't mean navigating this life will be easy. We will still have to fight to have a right perspective; however, the return of Jesus does mean that we have a hope in which to find perspective.

In 2014, we moved into a new house and were so excited. Well, we were excited until we found termite damage in a wall of our new home. It was horrible. My initial emotions were all over the map. I didn't know what to do or who to call. I'm not much of a carpenter or handyman. While ultimately a gracious man in our church ended up coming over and managing the entire ordeal for me, I didn't know at first how it would work out or the extent of the damage. As my mind raced, three thoughts comforted me and steadied my anxiety. One, this event didn't catch God off guard. Two, all this world will one day be destroyed. Three, I've got a home awaiting me that can't be damaged by termites. And God was so good to us. Almost immediately after settling down and trusting him, we saw him begin to bring glory to his name through this difficulty. We had opportunities to share a little more about our faith with our neighbors. People unexpectedly called to tell us God had placed us on their hearts, and they wanted to make sure everything was okay.

The reality of Jesus' future return can bring perspective to help us live confidently in this uncertain world.

Second, we see that anticipating Jesus' return should motivate us to walk in obedience to God. A deep belief that Jesus will return at any moment, coupled with an understanding that Jesus wants us to live rightly, should motivate us to live in such a way that we might be found faithful at his return. We want to be found doing what our king called us to do when he returns. Let's use a common occurrence in our public schools as an example. Imagine you are a teacher. You've been teaching sixth grade for three years and feel pretty confident doing so. Tuesday afternoon the principal calls to inform you that she will be sitting in on your third-period class tomorrow. How might her presence as the principal impact your performance? Well, you would certainly want to ensure you were on time, the class was clean, and you were prepared. Knowing her presence would make you more alert and motivated in the day's duties. Doesn't that make sense? In the same way, when we believe Jesus could return at any moment, we are more motivated to make sure we are not doing anything that would embarrass us or dishonor him. No one wants to be caught being stupid by the authority figure over them, and no one plans on being caught. I certainly didn't. I was in the eleventh grade. I was in typing class, and we had a big written exam coming up, which I thought was a waste of time and energy. After all, it's typing class. Why are we taking written exams? Shouldn't our grade be based on typing? Since I didn't agree with this whole process, I decided to cheat on the exam. I knew it was wrong, but I justified my decision. The irony is that I spent so much time preparing a cheat sheet I only needed on two questions out of the entire exam; nevertheless, when the teacher walked by, she saw it. The gig was up. I was busted. She gave me a zero on the exam, and I was embarrassed. If I had known she would catch me, I would have never cheated. That's the catch. No one in their right mind plans to be caught doing what they are not supposed to be doing. Jesus doesn't give us a clearer timeline on his return, party so we will seek to always live ready for his return.

Jesus wants us to walk in holiness in anticipation of his return. Now, for the believer in Christ, is your eternal salvation at stake? Certainly not! But, still, who wants to be in the middle of sin when their Savior returns? Moreover, if Jesus does not return during our lifetime, there will most certainly be a day in which we go to meet him. More likely than not, our death will not be an event we have scheduled. Consequently, we should consciously choose to live with the specific focus that sometime during our life we will unexpectedly meet our Savior and Lord.

Anticipating the return of Jesus motivates us as believers to "be" ready.

- ❖ Be the spouse you are called to be despite whether or not your spouse will change. Be the person you are called to be in a non-judgmental, compassionate, patient, and loving way.

- ❖ Be generous and start giving to the church in accordance with the prompting of God in your heart.

- ❖ Take a chance and invite that friend, neighbor, or co-worker to church. Don't put it off.

- ❖ Fight against the cultural pressure to neglect your family for your career. Begin to back off work a little in order to specifically invest in your family now. Tomorrow isn't promised. Be the parent you know God is calling you to be, even if it means moving, downsizing, or passing on a promotion.

- ❖ Share Christ with your classmates at school. Student years are often the best time to see people come to faith in Christ.

In all of these instances, we are not striving to be "good for goodness' sake"; rather, we are striving to live in light of the glorious salvation we have received and the reality that our Savior is coming back for us. Our goodness doesn't save us, but it honors him.

For those reading this book who have yet to turn their life over to Jesus, I implore you, decide now while there is still time. Telling God you were not ready for his return will not work. God will not accept that you chose to disregard the revelation of his grace, that you weren't really interested in Jesus' return, or that you never really expect to meet him.

My responsibilities at church resulted in my wife's and my having to leave home suddenly one day while our family was getting ready to starting house cleaning. I looked at my children and told them they did not have to clean everything, but they had to make sure the living room was cleaned before we returned. They acknowledge my words and said they would have it done, but when I returned home, the room still wasn't clean. Irritated, I called all of them into the living room and asked them why? Their response that they didn't know I would be back so soon was not a sufficient excuse. At the end of the day, telling God, "I wasn't ready" will not work.

Refocusing

Just like the "Where's Waldo" character was designed to provide a focal point in his pictures of crowds, Jesus Christ and his return are to be a focal point to bring hope in the midst of any situation. Living through such a lens brings a dramatically different approach to life. It's hard work, but it's also liberating. Billy Graham once shared a story that relates to this point.

> A little child playing one day with a very valuable vase put his hand into it and could not withdraw it. His father, too, tried his best, but all in vain. They were thinking of breaking the vase when the father said, "Now, my son, make one more try. Open your hand and hold your fingers out straight as you see me doing, and then pull." To their astonishment the little fellow said, "O no, father. I couldn't put my fingers out like that, because if I did I would drop my penny." Smile, if you will— but thousands of us are like that little boy, so busy holding on to the world's worthless penny that we cannot accept liberation. I beg you to drop that trifle in your heart. Surrender! Let go, and let God have His way in your life.[54]

---

[54] Billy Graham, *Peace with God: The Secret Happiness* (Nashville: W Publishing Group, 2011), § 2553-2559, Kindle.

Like this young child, some of us hear the challenge to focus on Jesus and his return, we try to do so, and we honestly respond, "I can't." The reason we can't is because we are simultaneously trying to focus on our worldly attachments. We cannot focus in two directions simultaneously. We have to break our focus on one in order to rightly focus on the other. If we would break our attachment to this world and focus on the reality that Jesus is coming again, just think of all the heartache, all the distress, all that frustration, and all the depression that could be alleviated. If we would break our attachment to this world and focus on the reality that Jesus is coming again, just think of how much more prone we would be to say no to sin and say yes to those promptings of the Spirit in our lives. Living this way is transformational, so let's be a people who live with their eyes fixed on grace until Jesus returns or calls us home (Heb. 12:1–2).

Questions for Reflection

Have you faced moments of hopelessness? Was there an event or problem that brought you to this point?

How should the resurrection of Jesus change how we live today? Why was the resurrection so important?

Do you ever think about the return of Jesus? How does it impact our daily lives? In what circumstances is it most critical to remember that Jesus is coming back?

What are some practical ways we can keep the return of Jesus in mind?

Are you ready for Christ to return? Is there any aspect of your life you would want to change if you knew he was coming back tonight?

CONCLUSION

Back to Square One

You're nearing the end of Square One, and we hope you've been transformed by what you read. The truth is that, when we let God speak, there is no limit to how he might work. As authors, our goal has been to get out of the way and let God work. Only he can change hearts and save lives.

So, our first stop in the book was to introduce the Gospel. The wonderful truth is that Jesus Christ is the center of all that we do and think. Without his perfect life, his transformative teaching, his sacrificial death, and his resurrection, we would have nothing to say. But Jesus changed everything. Through him we can be forgiven. And, yet, forgiveness is just the beginning. Once we realize our forgiveness, we see that we stand justified and holy before God. Everything has changed. And now, our lives exist not to gratify our own desires but to glorify that God who saved us. We are a changed people, and changed people live changed lives.

Along with forgiveness, justification, sanctification, and a new identity, we saw that God provides power. We no longer have to live as slaves to sin. God enables freedom and equips us to fight against sin. All of these gracious blessings draw us into deeper allegiance to our Savior, who calls all of his followers to carry on his mission of reaching the world. We treat others with compassion and share the truth with all we meet. And when life becomes difficult, and we struggle in our walk, we find refuge in the church. The family of God is critical, and each of us plays a vital role. We are called to care for one another as we await the return of Christ. And in spite of the great pain we may experience—even sharing in the sufferings of Christ—we have hope that he will return and right every wrong. This life is only the beginning for those who believe in the Gospel of Jesus Christ.

Moving on to Square Two

In light of all you've read, maybe you're wondering what the next step looks like. What is square two? We can recommend several steps. As we said in chapter nine, the local church is your home base. If you haven't done so, find a family of believers who will teach and exhort you daily. Surround yourself with likeminded Christians who can benefit from the fruit of your life and who can catch you when you stumble. And reach the world together.

Another step is to learn to study the Bible. Acquire skills that will help you hear God speak through his Word. You can read books like *How to Read the Bible for All Its Worth* by Gordon Fee and Douglas Stuart. If you're especially hungry, you can enroll in a hermeneutics class in a local college or university. Another option would be to ask around at church and find someone to teach you the basics. Whatever route you take, dig into God's Word.

Finally, never forget the Gospel. The reality is that, while the content of this book is square one, the truth of these chapters is engrained in every aspect of the Christian life. The Good News changes our marriages. It impacts our reason to serve in the church, not out of obligation but from a heart of gratitude. The Gospel affects our finances. We give money to support the mission of the church and to bless those in need. Jesus' death and resurrection transform how we respond to tragedy, how we vote, and how we parent. For the follower of Jesus, the Gospel changes everything. So, don't forget what you've read. Live in it. And live it out.

Scripture Index

Made in the USA
Columbia, SC
25 June 2018